THE AGONY OF BELGIUM

The Invasion of Belgium;
August-December 1914

SIR FRANK FOX

UNIFORM

This edition published by Uniform, 2017
an imprint of Unicorn Publishing Group

Unicorn Publishing Group
101 Wardour Street
London W1F 0UG
www.unicornpublishing.org

Beaumont Fox, 37 St. James's Place, London SW1A 1NS
02076290981
www.sirfrankfox.com

2nd Edition, First Published by Hutchinson & Co.,
London 1915

ISBN 978-1-910500-85-9

Printed and bound in UK

CONTENTS

FOREWORD

Sir Frank Fox was a journalist, author and campaigner who espoused the cause of warning of the dangers of a major War in Europe as early as 1909.

His views coincided with those of the Morning Post and he was invited to join their staff.

In 1914 he was sent as their War Correspondent to be attached to the Belgian Army. As the tragic events of the German invasion unfolded he must have harboured mixed feelings about his prophecies coming to pass. He reported on the appalling events at first hand, and greatly admired the fight put up by the Belgian Army against impossible odds. He witnessed the results of atrocities against the civilian population, including women and children, and the cultural outrages at Louvain and elsewhere. His admiration for the resolve and conduct of King Albert I was unbounded. He became close to him during the retreat to Antwerp and was later decorated by him with the Order of the Crown.

However Fox fretted at being a non-combatant, and at the restrictions imposed upon him by the British authorities. It was thus a relief for him to get back to England to be commissioned into the British Army in late 1914 (it seems that he lied about his age, being over 40 years old). Posted to France, Fox was blown up during the Battle of the Somme and suffered severe injuries. During his convalescence in England he worked for MI7, but longed to get back to France. He pulled strings and somehow, despite the loss of most of his right foot, and having minimal use of his left arm (let alone profound deafness) he was posted to Haig's GHQ at Montreuil-sur-Mer, and worked in the QMG's Department in the run up to the final offensive against Germany. He was appointed OBE (Military) and was Mentioned in Despatches.

After the War had been won, he returned to Belgium to

accompany King George V and Field Marshal Lord Haig to the Military cemeteries.

King Albert I remembered that Fox had passed him a box of cigars at Antwerp. "I was going to replace it – but then thought you would be insulted, as your kindness would have been interpreted as a loan rather than as a gift!" It was King George V who, in recognition of the bravery and sufferings of the Belgian people, decreed that they alone could conduct their own annual Remembrance Service at the Cenotaph in London.

Fox was a prolific author, writing some 33 books including 5 relating to WW1 (The British Army at War; The Battle of the Ridges; GHQ – Montreuil-sur-Mer; The Royal Inniskillings in the World War; The King's Pilgrimage).

This book was first published in 1915 and provides a unique account of Phase I of the Great War. The bravery of the Belgians and allied forces is clear for readers to see in this eyewitness report of the invasion of Belgium.

Dr.Charles Goodson-Wickes

Dr.Charles Goodson-Wickes is Sir Frank Fox's great-grandson and his Literary Executor.

THE AGONY OF BELGIUM

CHAPTER I

THE POLICY OF TORTURE; BELGIUM BEFORE
THE WAR

IN the last town of refuge left to the Belgian people there rests as a memory of old, unhappy days the instruments of a religious persecution. The grim robes which the judge-executioner wore, the weapons of burning, of tearing, of stretching his victims are preserved in the torture-room whose old timbers still, when the wind is high over the marshy plains of Flanders, seem to re-echo the sighs, the groans, the shrieks of that dead century.

When I write *are* preserved, I should say rather *were* preserved until very lately. Today that room is stripped of robe and cowl and brazier and rack. In November it was thought that the Germans would enter the town, and the instruments of torture were hurriedly hidden away in a buried chest. Why? Was it that the fear existed that the sight of these means of cruelty would prompt the German invader to new efforts of "frightfulness?" Was it with the symbolical idea of showing the flight of the old and the inefficient before the new and the scientific; the modest retirement of a brazier which could roast but one man at a time, before this great modern German Army with its up-to-date equipment for the burning and sacking of whole cities? Or was it merely that the fearful relics had a value and should be hidden from a German Army which cannot be trusted to spare anything of public or private worth? Often I asked and never knew quite clearly.

The old torture museum with its means of brazing and tearing the human flesh in the effort to conquer the human mind will be restored, no doubt, when the tide of invasion has receded and Belgium is free again. Then the traveller coming on a fearful pilgrimage to the war scenes of 1914–15 may stand there by the side of the old rack and call up to his vision the Agony of Belgium.

The victim of the rack, helpless in its grip, had from his torturer the invitation to recant, to betray, before he had suffered anything but the agony of anticipation. Then, if he were steadfast, the penalty was not a swift death coming straight upon the glow and ardour of his heroic "No." One turn of the rack brought a quivering torture; and again the invitation to betray. If his mind remained firm, little by little its fortresses were sapped, with increasing savageness its citadel assailed. With every fresh pain came a fresh temptation to recant.

So it was with Belgium. The faithful courage with which she refused on August and to sell the pass so that one neighbour, who had been her pledged friend and her promised protector, should attack by a treacherous back-path two other neighbours, also her friends and protectors, did not end the test of her courage. After the first demand and the first blow came another demand with the threat of another blow and with the bribe of peace and ease for a word of betrayal. The nation was kept on the rack, the torture applied with more and more savagery in the effort to break down the first faithful and heroic "No." A new seizure of territory, another massacre, another sackage -after each the helpless victim was tempted with the demand: "Will you yield now? There is ease for you if you will."

For four months I have stood by the rack whilst the strength of the martyr ebbed away: heard the shouted "No" of Liége fade and fade until it came down to the barely-heard whisper of Ypres. But always it was "No," indomitably "No." During those four months of the torture of Belgium there have been incidents of cruelty which went beyond the relentless, the fiendish, and were actually bestial. But no incident could equal in "frightfulness" the cold, considered malignity which at every turn of the rack offered to the tortured victim surcease from agony at the price of treachery.

Germany pleads that the pass through Belgium to attack France was a necessity of her war policy. In no court of national honour could such a plea be accepted. If Germany were not strong enough to come against France by the open road, let her have waited. It is vain to attempt to justify a murderous assault upon a little friend to whom you have solemnly promised protection with the plea that it was necessary in order to help a treacherous attack on a powerful enemy. But after the initial wrong, after the decision to try to murder Belgium, it was a madness of hate and pride to decide to accompany the killing with torture, and to accompany every phase of the torture with a new invitation to play the traitor. That last was the unforgivable sin, an attempted outrage on the soul of a nation.

It failed. Belgium still whispers feebly "No," whilst her executioner trembles at the sound of the forces of relief thundering at his gates. But if the German plan had succeeded-as it must have succeeded if Belgium had not saved, during a century of worldly prosperity, a moral courage of heroic strength in her soul? If it had succeeded, what expiation could have ever wiped out the record of the infamy? Those martyrs who withstood to the last a Nero's cruelty won life by losing it and could bless their executioner as they died. But what of those who recanted and carried out of the torture chamber their twisted limbs to continue a shamed life?

It was to that fate Germany tried to drive Belgium; and it was the most wicked of her cruelties. Having decided to attack Belgium without a shadow of right, the German nation might have mitigated her guilt by following in the attack most strictly such humane rule as international law proposes. Instead, she conducted the war against Belgium with an extreme savagery that recalled the Huns of Attila. Yet that was not the final, the deepest infamy. The deepest infamy was reached in the constant invitation to the tortured victim to abandon her faith and save extremer pangs.

All the efforts of the German torturer failed. As to what gave to he Belgian people and their ruler the courage to withstand them, the human mind must confess its failure to understand, and must fall back for explanation on its belief in a sustaining and ruling Providence. Writing now, at a time when the high fame of Belgium has been established without fear of any criticism, it is possible to say that the national history of the people before 1914 did not indicate clearly that they were of the stuff of which martyrs are made. Europe knew them best as a people of an astonishing material prosperity, whose wealth and good ease of living had inclined them rather to a national *embonpoint*. Julius Cæsar had said that of all the Gauls the Belgi were the most brave; and in the Middle Ages the Low Countries showed a fine mettle of courage more than once. But the nineteenth and twentieth centuries, it was thought, had changed all that. Certainly German diplomacy so concluded, and reckoned confidently that if not its first, its second attempt to induce Belgium to betray France and Great Britain would be successful. That second temptation (after the first mild turn of the rack and before any massacres of civilians) was plausible enough to give to the Belgians an easy road to faithlessness, if faithlessness had been in their minds. But the reply was as sturdy as the temptation was contemptible.

THE OFFER:

"The fortress of Liége has been taken by assault after a courageous defence. The German Government regrets most deeply that in consequence of the attitude taken up by the Belgian Government against Germany such sanguinary encounters should have taken place.

Germany does not come into Belgium as an enemy; it is only due to the force of circumstances that she has been compelled, on account of the French military preparations, to take the grave decision of entering Belgium and occupying Liége as a *point d'appui* for her subsequent military operations.

"After the Belgian Army has, by a heroic resistance against greatly superior forces, maintained the honour of its arms, the German Government begs the King of the Belgians and the Belgian Government to save Belgium from the subsequent horrors of war. The Government is ready to come to any agreement with Belgium which can be reconciled with its differences with France. Germany again solemnly declares that she has no intention of seizing Belgian territory, and that such an intention is far from her thoughts. Germany is at all times ready to evacuate Belgium as soon as the state of hostilities permit."

THE REPLY:
"The proposal which the German Government makes to us reproduces the proposal which was formulated in the ultimatum of August and. Faithful to its international obligations, Belgium can only repeat the answer it gave to that ultimatum, particularly as, since August 3rd, its neutrality has been violated, a grievous war has been carried on in its territory, and the guarantors of its neutrality have loyally and at once answered her appeal."

Again and again the Belgian courage was proved as the cruelty of torture grew. To every temptation there was the same firm answer. The nation, which in the pride of its wealth gilded Gothic traceries of stone and which for generations had been credited with sloth of spirit, showed itself stark and faithful into the very shadow of death.

The Belgian people even – I speak now from the confidences of their leaders-showed, during this torture, the ultimate heroism of taking on their own shoulders some of the responsibility for the utter material ruin which fell upon their country. They were prepared in a measure to blame themselves that the strength of their material arm was not equal to the strength of their spirit. That fact must be considered in judging the Belgian heroism. It was the heroism of a people who knew that they were insufficiently prepared for war.

It would be unnatural if the British people did not look upon the Belgian Army sympathetically. Its courage in going out to meet the German Army recalls David withstanding Goliath or (to give an illustration nearer home) Brabo, who overcame the giant who once held the passage of the Scheldt at Antwerp. [The giant, it will be remembered, was so much a giant that he could pluck up great ships in his hand and destroy them. Brabo cut off the hand of the giant and flung it at that spot (Antwerpen, Hand-flung).] In such wise, Belgium took off a finger from the Mailed fist and saved for Europe those precious days of August, 1914. Great Britain, the real enemy aimed at by the German power, feels a warm gratitude, and that gratitude is manifested in her generous appreciation of an army which showed courage, address, and a "sporting" spirit. Nevertheless, at the outbreak of the war, Belgium was in no sense a military nation, a prepared nation, and was not ignorant of the penalties which threatened her for her good faith.

The Belgian nation, grateful to its heroic soldiers, is under no illusions that it had a perfect army at the outbreak of the war. It admits that it lived in a fools' paradise for too many years, and says that if it had listened to the voice of its wise leaders, Germany would have been met with a Belgian Army of 500,000 fully-trained men, and before they had yielded a mile of Belgian territory 500,000 French would have been at their side, and no sack of Belgium would have been possible.

Imagining herself safe behind treaties which a brutal invader treated literally as "scraps of paper," Belgium was content until 1909 with the old-fashioned sytem which had existed since 1830. There was a volunteer army and a conscript army recruited by lot.

On a certain day of the year all young men of nineteen were called to the town halls of their communes and had to draw lots. A high figure in the lottery ensured the "lucky" drawer against military service. A low figure made him a soldier. A middle figure left his fate undecided until it was settled how many recruits were needed for the year. This conscription system was made worse by the existence of means of purchasing out. The son of the rich man who drew an unlucky number could buy a substitute for about £70, and this substitute would serve in his place. Those who remember the old system recall to me the scenes on conscription day: the crowds of relatives around the lottery boxes, the rejoicings of those whose lads drew high numbers, the grief, almost the despair, of those drawn for service. It was one of the life objects of every thrifty peasant to have saved up £70, so that if his son drew an unlucky number he could buy a substitute.

It can be imagined that the morale of an army thus recruited was not good. Only the existence of a band of officers of the highest quality and of a most rigid discipline could have made such an army good. Neither condition was met. It was not then "good form" to be in the army, except perhaps in the cavalry, and, apart from the natural courage of the people, the Belgian Army at the beginning of this century had little merit. Weak in numbers, it was deficient in morale, for to serve in the army was counted a misfortune rather than a duty or an honour. The soldiers, thus "outcasts" in popular estimation, were indifferently treated as regards clothing, food and lodging.

The European crisis which culminated in the present war really began to develop at the time when Austria-the cat's-paw probably of Germany-tore up the Berlin Treaty and annexed Bosnia and Herzegovina. At the same time, the German shipbuilding programme was divulged, and it will be remembered that all Europe shivered with apprehension of the coming great war, and that even in England the nation's slumber was marked by an uneasy turning, whilst in other parts of the Empire, such as Australia and New Zealand, vigorous defence programmes were at once adopted. In Belgium the defence reform party won new strength. The rich and the agriculturist still opposed reform, arguing that Belgium was safe under the shadow of treaties.

But after the Agadir crisis their opposition crumbled away. In 1909 the first great reform was effected when the system of buying substitutes was abolished and it was enacted that each family should give one son to the defence of the country. In 1912 a further great reform put the Belgian Army on its present footing, and for the year 1914, yet another step forward had been contemplated, instituting real universal service with a standing *cadre*-very much on the lines advocated by Lord Roberts in England. The 1912 system provided for universal service with modifications. Exemptions were given to sons who had to provide for their parents, to those young men who had brothers still under the colours, to those who were the eldest of several little children, and to others. But the 1912 system, whilst not perfect, was good, and if the war could have been delayed two years longer, so that it could have been got into full working order, the Germans would have had a still harder task at Liége.

There is little doubt that the transition stage of the Belgian Army reorganization was one of the reasons guiding the German Government in dating the war for 1914.

Briefly, the law of 1912 provided for a modern system of drilling, housing, equipping the Army.

Recruiting was after this manner: Young men at nineteen had to register their names at their local town hall. In the month of

January following, they had – with the exceptions I have noted-to present themselves for medical examination. In July they received their mobilization orders, which called them to come to the depots after the harvest in September or October. At the depots they received their uniforms and went to the regimental headquarters. Some had had already a little drill at school or at the gymnastic societies which the Government encouraged.

Service was for fifteen months for infantry, and twenty-two months for cavalry and artillery.

In the year 1913, the Belgian Army had grand manoeuvres for the first time in its modern history. The scene of operations was the Belgian Luxemburg and the fortress area of Namur. The mistakes then made taught valuable lessons for the real campaign of 1914. Barracks accommodation, food, pay, and equipment were at the dawn of the war excellent. But an army started in 1912 is evidently not grown up in 1914. The war found the Belgian forces just feeling their feet. There was not a sufficient stock of active officers, and practically no reserve of officers. In the infantry specially the shortage of officers was serious.

On the other hand, the new system had encouraged a good morale in the men. The army was no longer "unfashionable", no longer "outcast." It had the spirit to do the wonders of Liége, Tirlemont, Antwerp. Its crack corps were good-such, for example, as the University Companies. In every town which had a university or a collegiate institution of university rank, there were companies of the "University Regiments." Students of good character and diligence were admitted to these companies and allowed to pursue their civil studies at the same time as they took their military training. This system survived from the 1909 law. It was subjected to severe criticism at the outset as being a "class privilege," and for a while it seemed as if it would not survive, and would not deserve to survive, the criticism. But the spirit of *noblesse oblige* came to its rescue. The young collegians set themselves to prove that if they had a privilege they would deserve it with special diligence. The University force became in truth a *corps d'élite*, and in the war it more than justified itself by courage and address, some of its companies fighting to the point of actual extermination.

The "sportsmen" of Belgium, to, proved a tower of strength. One day the King of the Belgians, speaking to an officer whom he had promoted on the field, added to his congratulations a playful reproach: "But I am always having to congratulate you. Before it was for your successes in sport. Now it is for your success in war." To another officer, in hospital with a wound, His Majesty, in announcing to him a decoration for his gallantry, referred again to the fact that in this war of heroic defence on the part of Belgium the "sportsmen" of the country had done nobly.

The King's interest in all forms of manly sport is great. He has a great admiration for the British character, and has the conviction that British manhood owes much of its good poise and equable strength to the devotion of young men to games. This is given as the reason for the fact that, as Crown Prince and as King, he set himself to encourage in every way possible football, running, riding, tennis, fencing, hockey, and other sports.

One particular instance has been cited to me of his active interest. When football was first played in the Belgian Army some question arose as to whether it was consistent with good discipline for officers and men to play in the same regimental team. The King took the first opportunity to allow it to be known that he saw no danger to discipline in such comradeship. The event justified his good judgment.

Regimental football with officers and men playing side by side became a most popular feature of Belgian military life, and it certainly has not proved injurious to discipline. On the contrary, it has helped to an appreciation of comradeship in arms, and the "Football Regiments" have distinguished themselves in the field. (All the football in Belgium is "soccer," under strict amateur conditions.) Those young men of Belgium who were most prominent in manly sports before the war were most prominent in leadership of the nation's army. I met them in all capacities in the army; as officers, as privates-doing cavalry scouting, bicycle scouting, flying, running armoured trains and armoured motor-cars. Trace up some particularly dashing deed and one was almost certain to find that the man behind the gun learned his dash and ardour in some field of sport.

But, with all its good points, the Belgian Army was not a

trained military machine; and I have taken some pains to give an exact idea of its training as a necessary preface to this account of its operations; and also as necessary to an understanding of the degree of heroism which brought Belgium into the great European war on the side of good faith, and kept her firm during such horrors as have never before in modern history overwhelmed a nation. Belgium was not in the position of a Spartan nation trained to endure, to fight. She was a rich, plump, comfortable nation, "soft" to all outward seeming. But beneath the softness was a core of noble metal which has sustained her with unblemished courage and honour through an Agony which it is almost impossible for the man who was not a spectator to imagine, which I can scarcely realize, though I stood within the torture chamber during four terrible months.

CHAPTER II

ON July 31st, 1914, the mobilization of the Belgian Army was ordered, and the Belgian King at the same time called publicly Europe's attention to the fact that Germany, Great Britain and France were solemnly bound to respect and to defend the neutrality of his country. On August 2nd, Great Britain and France having replied that they would faithfully observe their treaty obligations, Germany intimated to Belgium that she intended to march troops through her territory to attack France, and if Belgium would acquiesce in this, then Belgium would not be annexed after the war and no damage would be done.

On August 3rd Belgium replied that to assent to that would be to sacrifice her national honour and to betray her duty to Europe, and on August 4th the Belgian King, addressing his Parliament, said:

"Never since 1830 has a graver hour sounded for Belgium. The strength of our right and the need of Europe for our autonomous existence make us still hope that the dreaded events will not occur. If it is necessary for us to resist an invasion of our soil, however, that duty will find us armed and ready to make the greatest sacrifices. If a stranger should violate our territory, he will find all the Belgians gathered round their Sovereign, who will never betray his Constitutional Oath. I have faith in our destinies. A country which defends itself wins the respect of everyone and cannot perish. God will be with us."

The same day the German Army violated Belgian territory, crossing the frontier at dawn. On August 4th Liége was attacked and on August 7th fell.*

* I did not arrive in Belgium until August 5th, and saw nothing of the operations around Liége. My knowledge of them is derived from statement: by officers, soldiers and citizens who were in the city. It is with some reluctance that I have decided to include in this book-intended to be a record of my direct personal observation-a chapter on Liége. But it was necessary to make the record of the Agony of Belgium complete.

Those who have followed the records of the war in the newspapers will be surprised at these dates. Late in August it was possible to read official assurances that the Liége forts were still holding out though the town itself had been occupied. In a great war such as the attack on Belgium opened, it is by almost universal consent that exactness of record is sacrificed temporarily when the military authority considers that such sacrifice is necessary. It was thought necessary to encourage the Belgian Army and people by withholding the truth about Liége; and to this plan of concealment all were parties except the German Government, whose interest it was to trumpet the victory over Liége, but who showed on its own part an economy of truth by concealing the serious checks which prefaced the victory.

The exact truth is that the Germans in their attack on Liége made an initial grave miscalculation and tried to "rush" the fortified position without adequate artillery preparation; were defeated with heavy loss; brought up fresh troops and their famous siege guns; and then soon captured the town and forts. There has been published in the *Belgian Army Gazette* a letter from General Leman, the heroic defender of the fortress, to King Albert which tells in skeleton form the story.

"SIRE, – After honourable engagements on August 4, 5 and 6 by the Third Division of the Army, reinforced on August 5 by the fifteenth Brigade, I considered that the forts of Liége could only play the rôle of *forts d'arrêt*. I nevertheless maintained military government in order to co-ordinate the de fence as much as possible and to exercise moral influence upon the garrisons of the forts.

"Your Majesty is not ignorant that I was at Fort Loncin at noon. Sire, you will learn with grief that the fort was blown up yesterday at about 5.20 p.m., the greater part of the garrison being buried under the ruins.

"That I did not lose my life in that catastrophe is due to the fact that my escort, composed of Commandant Collard, a sub-officer of infantry, who has undoubtedly perished, the gendarme Thevenin and my two orderlies, Vanden Bossche and Jos Lecocq, drew me from a position of danger where I was being asphyxiated by gas from the exploded powder. I was carried into a trench, where a German captain named Grüson gave me drink, after which I was made prisoner and taken to Liége in an ambulance.

"I am convinced that the honour of our arms has been sustained. I have not surrendered either the fortress or the forts. Deign, Sire, to pardon any defects in this letter; I am physically shattered by the explosion of Loncin.

In Germany, where I am proceeding, my thoughts will be, as they have ever been, of Belgium and the King. I would willingly have given my life the better to serve them, but death was denied me."

If that letter is dated August 8th (as published it was undated) it gives the outline of the story of Liége. The first actual attack on the town was made on the night of August 5th, and cost the German force great losses. The German left attacked Fort Fleron, and the interval between Fort Fleron and Fort Chaudfontaine; the German right attacked Fort Burchon, and the German centre Fort Evegnée. A small German force contrived to penetrate through the intervals between the forts and to enter the town. But this raid was beaten off after some street fighting. During August 6th individual forts were carried and on that night the town was entered, and from the park of the town next morning the fire of great howitzers directed on to the remaining forts, which were quickly destroyed.

Assurances continued to be given for many days afterwards that the Liége forts still stood. These I did not credit at first, and on August 7th wrote from Brussels:

"There is no definite announcement at the time I write, in the forenoon of August 7th, that Liége is in the hands of the Germans. But its fall is an event which may be presumed in an examination of the position. Allow now that the road is clear for them to pass south-west towards the French frontier, leaving Namur on their right flank, and all that can be said for them is that they have done in days what they expected to do in hours.

"That the reports of the numbers of troops engaged has been exaggerated by the Brussels press may be presumed. Nevertheless, it was a magnificent achievement, this holding of Liége, a civil town protected by forts, but not a fortress in the real sense. The Belgians seem to have had engaged one Army Division, and the Germans are reported to have employed three Army Corps, the 7th, 9th and 10th. I cannot warrant the figures.

"How the grand strategy of the campaign will be affected by this delay of three days at Liége I leave to others to judge. The local effect has been excellent. The Belgian troops, who at the outset were reminded by their King that the Belgians were the bravest of all the Gauls, have been much heartened. When a more serious effort is made to stand in the path of the Germans, an effort in which the French will take part, the effect of the good work of these early August days will be felt.

"There is no doubt that the Germans thought that they could trample over the Belgians. Today they can hardly hold that view, and the Belgians, with the plaudits of the French and Russian generals resounding in their ears, pre-pare to show themselves as good as the Germans, if not better.

"If one might look into the mind of the enemy at this juncture, it would probably be found that German diplomacy would wish to propose new and better terms to the Belgians, in the hope of securing even now a peaceful right-of-way; for it is already plain that they have miscalculated the strength of Belgian resistance, and must face a serious danger in leaving a confident and exasperated force on their flank, even supposing that they win the battle which must take place between Liége and Tournai, and pass on into France. But if German diplomacy should think of that, it would find probably that the German soldiery had made it impossible. Allowing all discount for the heat of their indignation deflecting Belgian accounts from the strictest path of accuracy, it is plain that the great European war has opened under circumstances of cruelty and remorselessness which augur badly for the populations within the area of the war.

"Putting aside as 'not proven' the accusations of actual infringement of the laws of war on the part of the Germans, yet they certainly have enforced the law with a rigour recalling the Franco-German campaign. War has in nothing ameliorated since then, judging by the record this past week of villages burned, of civilians executed for irregular attacks on troops. A reflection of the German rigour is given by the announcements from the civil authorities in all the Belgian towns, imploring citizens who are not authorized soldiers to refrain from any acts which might be called resistance to the German advance.

"But it will be difficult to secure full obedience to these wise warnings. The rage of the Belgian people, attacked so grossly without pretext, without warning, in defiance of all international law, is intense, and as it comes into direct contact with the German invaders will have a tendency to be uncontrollable. Until the Germans are thrown back on their frontier, this corner of Europe will flow with blood, not only of the soldiers, but of the civil population.

"The city begins to receive the wounded from the front. The great processions through the streets are dolorous, but they not dismay the people. For an English correspondent it is painful, however, to hear from the men the question: 'When will the English be here?' and from the women the assurance to their children: 'But soon the English will be here.'

"Today I have seen some of the chiefs of the General Staff. They have, of course, no illusions on the subject of the amount of help which can be hoped for. But they are confident. It is clear that the conduct of the troops has gone beyond their anticipations, and that on their plan of campaign they are doing better, much better, so far, than they had anticipated. But Belgium must look forward to a miserable month, trying to hope only that Europe will make it all good one day, when international law is respected again."

That was a correct appreciation of the position as it was then. Subsequently, the very strong assurances given that certain of the Liége forts still held out were accepted, though it was difficult to reconcile them with the actual developments of the German invasion then going on.

It is one of the difficulties of a war correspondent that he often finds a conflict between his pride in being well-informed and intelligently reading a position on the one hand, and on the other hand his patriotic duty to "play the game" of the friendly army that he is with. Of course the patriotic duty must take precedence even of correctness. Hence the public must not expect, either in official *communiqués*, or in the despatches of the most careful war correspondents, "the truth, the whole truth, and nothing but the truth" about a current operation. That can only be told, in most cases, after the lapse of some little time. The true history of a war cannot be told day by day.

One remarkable incident of the attack on Liége only came to my knowledge some weeks later, when there arrived at Antwerp a body of the old Liége field force. Their story was wonderful. They related that at the outbreak of the war their post was between the forts of Chaudfontaine and d'Embourg. They belonged to the First Battalion of the 34th Regiment. On the Wednesday night of the first week of the war (August 5th), orders were given to the field force to evacuate its position. The orders never reached this battalion, which did not retire and found itself isolated amidst the German Army, but with a strong fort on each flank. The Germans were aware of their presence, but seemed puzzled as to their actual strength and contented themselves with reconnaissance attacks, which the battalion bravely beat off.

The Belgians entrenched themselves, and for days and nights after the retirement of the main field force actually held the position.

They slept in the trenches under arms, and were fed chiefly by peasants, who brought them beer and cakes. They also had a few oxen, and with beer and flour they made a kind of bread. Under these marvellous circumstances the five hundred kept the field, repulsing constant German attacks. Heavy German artillery came up against the forts and shells showered on the little camp, but the men had dug themselves in well. finally, food becoming short, they decided to try to break through the German lines. They passed south along the valley of the Ourthe, found the bridge at Tilff destroyed, searched out a ford, crossed, and took shelter in the little wood of Sart Tilman on the western side of the river.

They then turned towards Boncelle, but that was going back to the lion's mouth, for the Germans surrounded that fort. The adventurous company had imagined that only the eastern forts were attacked. Still courageous, they passed west, taking advantage of the friendly woods, and reached the village of St. Lambert, which was occupied by Germans, but not in force. Separating, the Belgians managed to steal through the German patrols, and, re-uniting, came to a decision to throw themselves into one of the Belgian forts if possible. They got near Loncin Fort, but found themselves again surrounded by masses of German troops. A slight action followed, and some ten men were wounded.

The heroic band held a council of war, at which a proposal for surrender was rejected, and they decided to make another effort to break through. The wounded were left behind in charge of the Red Cross detachment, and the battalion marched towards the forts of Hollogne and De Flémalle.

Fortune favoured the brave, and they reached in safety Seraing, in the direction of Huy, where they expected to find a friendly force. Instead, they encountered patrols of German cavalry, whom they fought and put to flight, taking some prisoners, who told them of the presence of German cavalry near by. They avoided them and reached Huy on August 23rd after a forced march of sixteen hours, on the way with German patrols.

At Huy another disappointment awaited them, for the Belgian forces had left, and the Germans were hourly expected by the railway stationmaster. But he managed to make up a train quickly to get them to Namur, and thus ended eighteen days' fighting and marching. Two days later Namur fell, and these Liége soldiers found refuge in Antwerp.

On August 9th the survivors of the Liége field Army – the Third Division and the fifth Brigade – were reviewed at Brussels by King Albert, and congratulated on their heroic defence of the city. The Belgian army – three precious days having been saved by the Liége garrison and the outpost troops – was now hurrying into position to delay further the German advance.

CHAPTER III

PLAYING FOR TIME

AFTER the fall of Liége, the Germans renewed their proposal to Belgium to allow them a free road. The proposal was rejected and the Belgian Army took up a position along the line between Antwerp and Namur, with Lonvain as its centre and Tirlemont as its advanced base of operations. Using with great skill the thick network of railways covering the country, the Belgian command managed to secure some days of delay which were of great value to the French mobilization and the transport of the British force to the Continent.

It would be tedious to attempt to chronicle all the series of little engagements which marked this stage of the campaign. Let me describe one on August 9th, 10th, 11th (Sunday, Monday, Tuesday) at Grindt, near Tirlemont.

The scene of the operations was a low ridge running parallel with a line of railway, the fields broken by little copses of trees and the spires of two churches flying the national flag. In the fields the wheat was gathered up into stooks, which gave some cover. The position was held by a mixed brigade of infantry and cavalry, with three batteries of artillery. The operations opened on Sunday, when the cavalry of the enemy came into touch with ours. The Belgian cavalry proved itself at first contact superior to the German, and forced it back, but when the Belgian cavalry followed up this successful opening with a charge, the Germans suddenly brought up mitrailleuses, and there were many casualties among the Belgian horse. This unfortunate incident in no way disturbed the Belgians. The cavalry retired with composure on its supports. The infantry and artillery came into action on the Belgian side, and the Germans retreated. That night and during Monday all arms were engaged, and the Belgians held their position with complete success.

On Monday evening the Germans developed a heavy artillery fire on the Belgian entrenched infantry.

For the development of the plan it was necessary later for the infantry to change their position under the fire of the German artillery, and they did this with but little loss. The Belgian artillery officers spoke at this stage with little respect of the German gunners. Throughout Monday night and Tuesday morning the engagement continued without any change of fortune, every German attack being beaten off with loss. It was then signalled to the Belgian force by their scouts that large artillery reinforcements were coming up on the German side but they did not arrive. Late on Tuesday evening our cavalry scouts reported their front clear of the enemy.

What had happened in effect was that the Germans had developed a reconnaissance in force on this, the south side of Tirlemont, had been met strongly, and decided that that road was too well held. I recorded that night:

"The scene today on the field gave at once painful and joyous impressions. It was painful to see this fruitful country, gleaming golden with its rich wheat in the summer sun invaded thus without cause by a destroying enemy; it was joyous to see the Belgians marshalled in their cornfields under the shadow of the spires of their churches to beat back the enemy. They were so confident, so happy; there was not a trace of doubt. It was a battle *au picnic* judging by the attitude of the men. I stood behind one of the batteries ready for action amid the stooks of corn, the observing officers being mounted on tripods which gave them a view across the brow of the ridge; officers, men, and horses were marked by a steady content. There was no suggestion of fatigue nor of the harshness of battle. They had lost some good comrades, in the cavalry especially, but they had beaten back the enemy and were waiting for him to come again to beat him again.

He did not come, and I saw the greater part of the Belgian force march away to its cantonment serenely joyful. Perhaps during the night they would be called upon to give battle again, certainly the next day, but what mattered? This one unit of the wall of men standing against the invader had succeeded in its week's work, and the next day could be looked to with confidence.

"Apart from the steadiness, cheerfulness, and good equipment of the men, I was much impressed by the clever manner in which the work was handled from staff headquarters.

If the army behaves as well and is as well handled along the whole line, the German advance should be checked for some days."

The next day, August 12th, I recorded:

"Almost one begins to hope that this place, where the advance posts of the Belgian Army stand in rank, will prove to be the scene of a coming great battle. I had expected it much further south-west, but so astonishing has been the success of the Belgian arms in encounters during reconnaissance that it is possible now to hope for what would have seemed a miracle a fortnight ago. Of course, the German mass has yet to move, but every hour of the delay which has been imposed upon it has been equivalent to a defeat, and it does really seem that it still remains a blind mass and must unroll its plan of battle before it has learned how our forces disposed to meet it. Everywhere along the line of outposts the Germans meet with baffling checks. Like an angry dog faced by a porcupine with bristles, defiant at every point, the vaunted Prussian Army stands puzzled.

"Today I have traversed some twenty kilometres of our front and have visited three positions. Except for the reply of guns to a feeble German artillery attack near the centre of the section of the front I explored, I have seen no fighting. The right wing had faced an attack with all arms at the dawn, and, as usual, had repulsed it without, as I learned from some of the officers engaged, disclosing anything as to the real position. I do not wish to exaggerate the facts and to pretend that the Belgian force is winning a series of important battles. The successes are all intrinsically small successes, but they are making a habit of success. All dread of the Prussians has gone. That is a most valuable gain, apart from the fact that the German effort to search out our dispositions seems to be failing.

"I visited Grindt where I had seen the operations on Tuesday. The Germans had been satisfied with their repulse on Monday and Tuesday and had made no further attack. I am as certain as possible that here they had learned nothing except that the Belgian lion has strong claws. From there I passed a little behind the outpost front to a position near Tirlemont where the Germans had attacked this (Wednesday) morning. They had been repulsed. The Belgian loss was slight. Then I went to the extreme left of the section, where nothing had been attempted by the Germans. Then, guided by the sound of cannon, I went to the centre. Here a desultory exchange of shots between the Belgian and German artillery was taking place. The following morning an attack in force was expected.

"As I left the field at sunset to make my way back to Brussels, in the luminous afterglow of the summer evening the gay Belgian soldiers were at their supper. From every hamlet there stole up lines of old men, of women, of children bringing up comforts for the troops. Laughter crackled, cheerful jokes passed in the last of the light. Side by side with guns and entrenchments a few old and young people still toiled at the harvest, gathering in the wheat lest the invader should in trampling it on the morrow.

"Returning to Brussels, which is quietly sleeping, I wonder when the German military skill will begin to show itself. So far there has been nothing shown. The audacity of the Uhlan raids has on test come down to nothing more than audacity of bewilderment, the blind rush of men pushed on from behind. In contact with the Belgian cavalry they have shown themselves inferior. The German artillery has not shown brilliancy, nor the infantry. Perhaps there is something wonderful to be disclosed when the flood is let loose and the hundreds of thousands swarm into Belgium, but so far nothing."

The next day, early in the morning at Haelen in the north and at Eghezee near Namur, German attacks developed and in both cases were beaten off. At the battle of Haelen, which I witnessed, the Belgian position was as a triangle based upon a railway line, and with its apex pointed north-east. This apex was to be held by entrenched infantry, supported by one battery of artillery. The intention was, if a heavy German attack developed, to draw in towards the base of the position. The German attack, however, came in unexpected form, a cloud of cavalry being followed by strong artillery forces, which shelled the Belgian infantry heavily. For the infantry to leave the trenches would have exposed it to heavy loss in retiring, and would have left a way open to the Germans. The order was given to hold the position to the last, and it was obeyed.

The battalion suffered severely until the Belgian artillery came up and engaged the guns of the enemy. Then the battalion left the trenches, not to retire but to attack the German artillery. A general engagement followed, in which the Germans were emphatically worsted. The troops rested on their arms during the night, and at dawn the Germans sought to advance again. It was a half-hearted attempt, and was soon repulsed. The Germans were able to carry away their wounded with them.

Their losses were great. It is officially computed that the number engaged on either side was about 6,000 and that the German losses were half of their total. Except in the opening phase of the engagement the Belgian loss was slight. A very large proportion of the casualties were, however, of officers.

This was the case in all the early engagements, as there was practically no reserve of officers, the Belgian Army-in the infantry particularly-began to suffer a loss of morale from the lack of company officers.

On August 16th, I recorded (it will give the best idea of the war at this stage if these day-today impressions are set down as they were made, even when the subsequent events proved them too optimistic):

"I was able yesterday to traverse the *terrain* of our defensive positions in the north with a cavalry officer in charge of a scouting party. The tour made much clearer the course of the past week's operations, which may be summarized as repeated German attacks with cavalry and mitrailleuses, sometimes, particularly at Haelen, combined with considerable infantry and artillery. Generally, however, the engagements were with cavalry only. The Belgians were successful invariably on the north line, from which direction an attack on Brussels was feared, and it was perfectly clear that up to Saturday evening no strong German attack had developed. There is no immediate danger for Brussels, the Germans doing no more than feeling for our left flank or making the feint of an attack. It is on the south that the main German advance will develop, and there is good news this morning that the French have pushed back a strong reconnaissance attack south of Namur towards Dinant. The Germans were driven towards the fort of Dave with loss.

"Events must now march quickly. There is good reason for the optimism shown at headquarters, for it is pointed out that it has taken eight days for the German advance guard to get to Hasselt on the north and Hannut on the south. It is calculated that four German army corps will be engaged in the attack, with a fifth holding the lines. The position of the Germans seems already embarrassed, and a defeat next week would make it difficult. If, on the other hand, the Belgians and allies have to fall back, there is no reason at all for despair.

"The battlefield of Haelen had many peasant visitors yesterday, and a close examination of the position showed that the battle was really a notable success, proving Belgian coolness and resource amid difficulties. A cavalry officer tells me that the German cavalry charged with splendid courage. One squadron was left with five effectives, but still another squadron charged and still another. A letter found on a German officer at Haelen speaks in terms of high praise of the Belgians. He confesses to great surprise at their skill. The mitrailleuses are proving very effective on both aides. The Belgian mitrailleuses are drawn into action by dogs, which on the battlefield show complete coolness.

" My examination of the northern position led to an incident which illustrates the close watch for spies. I entered an *estaminet* near Orsmael and asked for coffee.

The proprietor sent a little boy to acquaint the guard that a German spy had come, 'because I spoke so strangely' (his speech being Flemish *patois*). While drinking my coffee I was interrupted by finding a pistol on each side of my head. I was confronted with eight eager young Belgians panting for an execution. Rather foolishly I reached for my papers instead of putting my hands up, almost with fatal consequences. Ultimately explanations were forthcoming, followed by apologies and protestations of friendship. A great variety of *patois*: is spoken in the various districts. The effacement of all signboards makes travelling difficult. The Belgian cyclists are proving very thorny to the German cavalry on this *terrain*, which resembles closely that of Sussex. It is reported that the cyclists are so effective that the Germans have announced they will give them no quarter, but that is unconfirmed.

The war at this stage was a cyclists' and an automobilists' war. The horse was forced into an inferior place. As war correspondent I found the cycle the most useful of equipment. It is, I suppose, quite against the rules of the game to follow military operations on a bicycle. But probably the game of war correspondent can hardly ever be played again in the grand manner, with full credentials, a baggage train, and a team of horses. Times and conditions have changed. After this experience with the Belgian Army I give a reliable bicycle the palm over horses or motor-cars as an aid to getting about country in war time. It can go wherever there is a vestige of a road or a track. It is not difficult to carry over fences and through fields to get into the actual line. It asks for no food except an ounce of oil every 100 miles. It excites the least attention from friend and I have been within smell of the Uhlans repeatedly on a bicycle, and have been accepted evidently as a civilian inhabitant of the country without challenge. In the motor-car I should have to stop for examination or face the chances of a volley. Within friendly lines an officer can wink at a bicycle going unobtrusively through his troops when a motor-car would have stopped because of the general attention it would attract. General attention means the general's attention, and he may not wink at a friendly journalist's enterprises. Further, a cycle – given good wind in the rider and fair surface – can do its 75 miles a day, and always it can take advantage of a bit of railway or tramway help, or be loaded up on a motor-car for a stage.

My bicycle, the best quality of a well-known English brand, has been now to two wars. I got it as far as Kirk Kilisse in the Balkan campaign, and it proved useful at a pinch, not adding much weight to the ox-wagon's load when the surface was hopeless, often giving a chance of a speedy twenty miles to see

some interesting point. In Belgium, where the people had the
cool habit of running the railways along almost to the battle
front in places, the cycle was of noble value. It was all I took
out with me in the retreat from Brussels (to anticipate a little),
and if, going out, I had been offered a seat in a motor I would
have refused unless the bicycle could have come too. It was
the one absolutely sure means of quick transport. To get from
Brussels to Terneuzen between 11 a.m. and 7 p.m. was a fair
achievement. And if, as had been anticipated, there had been
some attempt to hold the Brussels suburbs against the enemy
the only way to have seen the fighting and to have got out safely
would have been by cycle.

Experience with a motor showed that it was stopped long
before it was near to the actual operations.

My bicycle, through the whole Belgian campaign, got only one
firm refusal to pass, and that was over a section of road which
had been mined. As, too, it was a palpably English bicycle, a
massive "dragoon" type of machine, it served almost everywhere
as a passport. Soldiers would recognize it as "anglaise," and
those who knew a little English would call out, "Good day!"
"Good luck!" "What cheer!" and little groups would give cheers
for England.

For helping the operations, as well as for seeing operations,
the bicycle has proved of great value in this war. In scouting, the
Belgian carabineer cyclists have been able to outmanoeuvre the
German cavalry patrols. A Belgian cavalry officer, Lieutenant
Raoul Daufresne, 3rd Regiment Lancers, confessed to me
reluctantly that for scouting work the bicycle had proved better
than the horse. He is a very distinguished horseman, well
known in London, who has been complimented by our King
on his riding at the Horse Show, and love a horse as much as
he loathes a bicycle. But experience has taught him the cycle's
value, and in proof of his faith he came out with me one day
mounted, not on a horse, but a cycle. From him I learned the
probable explanation of some early German atrocities. The
carabineer cyclists, travelling along side-roads, and finding
the German cavalry patrols careless and reckless, were often
able to ambush them. On one occasion six carabineer cyclists
ambushed twenty-two Uhlans and killed most of them. Those

who escaped took back news that they had been attacked by civilians-probably an honest mistake on their part-and a large force of Uhlans returned and exacted a terrible reprisal on the village. It was here they hanged one of the carabineer cyclists who had fallen into their hands.

CHAPTER IV

BRUSSELS: THE FLOOD BREAKS

FROM the first day after the fall of Liége a German threat was held out against Brussels. On the 11th August, indeed, a great body of German cavalry was reported to be massed at Tongres, ready for a swoop on the capital. The city, which during the first days of the war had had an excusable spasm of wild flurry (the excitement showing chiefly in spy-hunting), had settled down to quietness again with the reassurance given by the heroic defence of Liége, and did not show any serious return of apprehension until the enemy was almost at its gates. Most of us had a confidence that the German invaders would have the good policy to spare Belgium as much as possible, and would therefore break as narrow a track as circumstances permitted through her defences.

Such a policy would have left Brussels on one side, and possibly have contented itself with masking Namur.

We had miscalculated the German mind. Throughout this great war the German nation has shown an absolute incapacity to appreciate or to make allowance for any but the ruthless military point of view of a situation. In particular, Germany has never shown any capacity to be a gentleman and to show a gentleman's feeling towards an opponent. With a more skilful diplomacy Germany would have resolutely refused to be goaded into any actions against Belgium which were not strictly necessary to ensure a safe path. In the long run that would have proved the least expensive course from a military standpoint; and it would have had the additional advantage of leaving still open the way to resuming diplomatic negotiations with her enemies in the field if that should prove advisable. Germany, however, pursued a policy of blind brutality and shaped her campaign in Belgium as if she were suppressing in a rage the treacherous revolt of an ungrateful province instead of invading a friendly neighbour to serve a momentary military convenience.

Whether it was a military necessity or not to occupy Brussels, the Germans clearly were resolved to do it as part of a stern lesson that was to be taught to the Belgians for daring to keep faith. But up to the night of August 18th it was reasonable to hold the hope that Brussels would escape an attack in force and occupation, though it was felt that raids of Uhlans were possible. As a precaution against these some rough defences were set up around the city-trenches, barbed-wire entanglements, and pits. Some sections of roads entering the city were covered with broken bottles. In at least one place the night before the occupation snow from the city's ice stores was spread on the streets, whether with the idea of making an obstacle or of getting rid of the stores of that summer comfort I could not ascertain. The improvised defences of the city were in the aggregate pathetically futile. They would have been of no possible use against an enemy with one battery of field artillery, but they were a source of grave annoyance to the peaceful citizens going in and out of the city.

On the 18th August the German flood broke with dramatic suddenness. The enemy developed an overwhelming attack on the Belgian front from Diest to Tirlemont. For almost a fortnight the small Belgian force, acting with great resource and energy (as I have shown), had kept the enemy puzzled and baffled, and had inflicted several minor defeats. On the 18th the Germans came with crushing force, and, despite a brave struggle, the Belgians were beaten back from position to position. Some accounts say the Germans had a superiority of ten to one. Certainly they were a vastly superior force. Diest was captured, Tirlemont was captured and in part set on fire. Throughout the night the tide of the German invasion flowed over Comptich, Roosbeck and Coorbeck-Loo. When, early on the morning of the 19th, I reached Louvain I found that the General Staff had departed with the government for Antwerp and that the University city was being evacuated by the civil population, whilst a horde of refugees streamed into it from all the villages to the east.

It was the beginning of the exodus of the Belgian nation, an exodus which continued throughout August, September, and October, and was not stayed until November, when, on the last poor little scrap of Belgian territory, the King led his troops to victory along the line of the Yser. The pitifulness of that exodus I cannot hope to describe adequately. It calls for a writer of epic power, and perhaps no one, however well equipped, would quite succeed, for the human mind becomes dulled, stupefied after witnessing many scenes of horror, and is incapable of recording impressions clearly. See for a whole day's journey crowds of refugees from sacked villages, and at the end of the day the mental impression is like that produced in photography by giving several exposures to one plate. There is a misty, confused record of great horror, but not a clear impression of details. Seeing a burned-out town once, one gets a sharp impression of indignation and grief. After seeing several, the sharpness of the impression is lost.

After four months in Belgium I have a dim and awful memory; in my ears of groans, of haggard silences more terrible than groans; in my nostrils of the charnel smell of houses which have been burned up with their inhabitants; and in my eyes of a mist of blood and smoke. The individual incidents standing out are, strangely enough, those trivial things which the mind grasps at for relief under the burden of seeing an intolerable misery; just as in a poignant melodrama some "comic relief," however poor, is eagerly welcomed.

Of the road into and through Louvain that morning of August 19th I can recall most clearly thoughts of the uselessness of a child carrying an empty bird-cage tightly clutched in its hand; of the folly of an old woman hugging desperately in her arms a very fat dog. I can remember that some people had put on their best clothes to flee, and their travel-stained gala dress gave to them the aspect of revellers coming distraught from a night festivity intemperately carried into the morning hours. Others had taken flight in their night clothes. Many carried useless things; others had methodical packs, which probably contained a wise selection of their household goods. Young children and very old people were dragged on by their sturdier relatives. The road was deep with dust, and sometimes child or grandparent would fall in the dust and be dragged on in wild haste. Cyclists rushed through the fugitives, knocking people down, being knocked down. When there were carts, usually they were filled with children and furniture, the adults tramping by their side.

Trivial things all! What escapes my poor power of record is the sense of the horror and the tragedy of the spectacle of these good, harmless people, set fleeing through blood and fire from their homes and fields, because of the mad ambition of some man or men utterly strange to them and their little lives, who did not even hear the bewildered cries with which they set out on their path of misery.

Scarcely less miserable than the sight of the civil fugitives was that of the Belgian Army, broken for the time being, in retreat along the road to Malines. It was clear to me then that the road to Brussels was open to the invader. The army now in retreat had done brave work, but for the present, as it drifted leaderless along the roads, it could not be rallied. Furthermore, its line of retreat was towards Malines and Antwerp, not to a position in front of Brussels.

I returned to Brussels, which was already a little uneasy at the stream of refugees arriving from Tirlemont, but which was not allowed to know the real position. The barbed-wire entanglements and entrenchments had been manned by the Civic Guard. They could have stopped raiding Uhlans, but against a brigade they were useless, and the city would have been subjected to scenes of horror and carnage if a defence were attempted. On every prominent citizen whom I could see I sought to impress the stern necessity of a policy of non-resistance so far as the city was concerned, and then turned my motor towards Namur, to see how it went with the defence of the citadel.

It will illustrate the dramatic suddenness with which the German flood broke on the 19th, if I reproduce a note from my diary of the previous evening regarding Namur. It reads:

"The position this evening, according to the official statements and my own observations made yesterday, remains good. I went yesterday along the Wavre-Gembloux line, and witnessed the defensive operations there, which were completely successful. Something of a scare was caused in the city by the news that Gembloux had been captured, but it was found to be only a raid. The Germans, obviously well served by spies, pounced on the town just after a troop of French cavalry had left, and destroyed the main railway lines. They were soon driven out, and the railway traffic from Brussels to Namur is likely to be resumed shortly. The Belgians run their railways with superb *insouciance* almost into contact with the enemy. After a raid the service is interrupted temporarily, but it is resumed on the first opportunity.

"None of the fighting at Namur is of real importance, except in so far as it damages German prestige and checks their search for our flank. All the indications point to the Germans having sought in vain for a gap, and they will, therefore, be forced to make a frontal attack on the Meuse line around Namur. A Belgian journalist, a correspondent of the *Peuple*, relates that, passing by the railway from Namur towards Dinant yesterday, the train went as far as Godinne. Both sides of the river from Godinne onwards were held by the French, but there was constant skirmishing with German cavalry.

"But on the afternoon of the 19th, it was impossible to get through to Namur, either by rail or by motor. In endeavouring to do so I nearly came to an end of my experiences as a war correspondent-and not by a German bullet!

"It was, I vow, a Civic Guard who led me into the trap. The French General of Division did not believe me, however, when I told him so in exculpation.

"'Ah! ' he said, with a smile breaking through his official mask of severity. 'Ah! I know you journalists!'

"He had been Military Attaché with the Russian forces in a recent war; and he knew the journalist's hunger for facts. All the same it *was* a Guard who was at fault.

I had rushed down from Brussels for a last peep at the fighting arena, knowing that Brussels was under the paw of the Germans, and would be seized that night or the next morning. On such an afternoon I was not likely to go, of my own wish, right into the middle of the headquarters of a French army division engaged in battle. With the Belgians, the trustful Belgians, you can take a little liberty. Provided they know you to be a friend they will give you a free leg; though they take good care to see that you are a friend. The French, when they are at battle, have (quite rightly) no time to see whether you are a friend or not. If you are caught on the field you are tied up until the battle is over, or you are shot, to make certain. The chances may be a hundred to one that you are all right; but when the issue of a battle may depend on a successful spy why should any general take that hundredth chance?

"Well, a Civic Guard at an outside village, tempted by the chance of a ride in a motorcar towards his home just when his duty was done for the day, offered to conduct me along; and because we had a Civic Guard in front, we had no challenges until we were right in the centre of the French cavalry headquarters. Then a Civic Guard who knew took charge. Would we please consider ourselves under arrest?

"Promptly I offered to go back. No, it was as impossible to go back as to go forward. We could, if we wished, find shelter under arrest in the house of the Mayor of the village until the French commander could have time to deal with us. I turned in with a shiver at the thought of missing the Brussels news.

When would a general of division find time to deal with a journalist and his chauffeur? What a remorse, anyhow, to think that one had taken a single moment of his time away from his task of beating the Germans!

"In the house of the Mayor the little plump wife of the Mayor greeted me with a look partly of consternation, partly of pity.

"'*Vous n'avez pas de bons papiers!*' There was a suggestion of the Last Trumpet and the Day of Wrath in the tone of her voice. A 'paper' character with us English is a term of contempt. *Bons papiers* are the very breath of life on the Continent, especially in time of war.

"I tried to reassure the motherly dame, telling her that truly I had excellent papers, was Anglais, was *bien affecté*, and that as soon authority came on the scene it would be all made clear.

"But she was not convinced. Had I not shown my papers to the Civic Guard commandant? And had he not put me under arrest? Then, truly my papers could not be good.

"I heard her explaining in the next room to someone that

the young man did not look like a spy, but he had not 'good papers.' And those words *'bons papiers'* were just like two tombstones, one for my head and one for my feet. I was as good as dead in the lady's mind.

"I think she thought I might be shot in her little *salon*, and she was distressed about the awkwardness of it all. Partly because of her distress, partly because of the urging to get back to Brussels for the German entry, I took a foolish resolution. I would leave the *mairie* and go to the military headquarters, in the hope of finding an officer who could deal with my *bons papiers* – indisputably *bons,* except for the fact that:

"(1) I had no right to be in the middle of a big French operation, and

"(2) the British Government had the previous day asked for the retirement of all British journalists from Belgium.

"I found a non-commissioned officer who was very civil: and he found a colonel who had just come back from pushing back Uhlans, and probably had not pushed them back far enough to satisfy his thirst for Berlin; and the Colonel dealt with me promptly by sending me with a couple of soldiers to the guard-room. He would not hear a word.

"The village concluded then that I *was* a spy, and gathered around the windows of the guard-room and made remarks and threats and spat. Soldiers crowded to the door, two of them flourishing revolvers, all of them menacing. I started to speak.

"They took aim. I shut up. 'Now,' said I to myself, 'it is your duty to look calm and collected and English and frank.' I thought a cigarette would help, and lit one-without being shot at-and then remembered that a villain always lit a cigarette when his infernal machinations were discovered: and discarded it; and concluded that that was a mistake too; and was acutely miserable, and heard as afar off a voice croaking *'Pas de bons papiers'* in a tone of doom.

"It was a good half-hour before deliverance came in the shape of an officer doing rounds, a very French officer of the Gascon type. I was tired of talking in bad French, which was taken to be German-French, and at a venture I called out to him:

" 'I swear you know English!'

" 'Why, yes. But what do you do here?'

It was fairly simple after that. I was cleared of suspicion of being a German, and was just, at the worst, an indiscreet English journalist. I explained that I was desolated to think of my silly little affairs worrying men who had big business on hand, but Brussels –

"He was interested to hear about what was going to happen to Brussels, and promised to go to the General at once. He did so; and brought me along. And, as the Fates would have it, that General knew me slightly personally, knew mutual friends well, chatted for five minutes, shook his head over my explanation of the 'accident' which brought me there; finally decided that, because it was quite certain that I was all right, and because it was not desirable to keep me away from Brussels that night, he would take special steps to get me safely there. There were certain formalities with the military police, who at first wished me to swear to divulge nothing, and then, on an explanation by the *sous-officier* who had come from the General, took my word of honour. But I got free in good time.

"But some time will pass before I forget that motherly dame and the doom in her voice:

"'Vous n'avez pas de bons papiers.'"

Returned to Brussels at nine in the evening, I found that negotiations during the afternoon had led to the decision not to defend the city. Preparations for surrender were going on, but this was kept from the citizens. However, news from Louvain had come in on the wings of rumour, and, despite the reassuring official statements, the real position was fairly well recognized.

There began a flight from the city, the most pathetic feature of which was that the refugees from Tirlemont who had sought refuge in Louvain, and had hurried on to the capital, had now to set out on a new flight. At ten o'clock the railway station was closed in face of the crowds of would-be travellers. There began then a wild rush for motor-cars and carriages. The main roads to the east were crowded with cars containing whole families.

Petrol was more precious than fine wine, and hidden stores of it were brought out and sold at famine prices. Through the night the rush continued, and as late as two in the morning I encountered hurrying along one of the magnificent Brussels boulevards, sixteen old people huddled up in a hay cart with some household goods, the younger generation of the families marching along holding on to the cart. It was a little village in flight! The German name indeed had been made terrible.

With great difficulty I secured for my own retreat a motor, whose driver wished himself to flee. My plan was to withdraw outside the city that night with the motor, then to return quietly on my bicycle and see the Germans in and cycle back to my motor at the last moment. There was trouble in getting petrol, which was being sought wildly on every side. Then the chauffeur insisted on bringing his wife and two dogs for flight.

Our retreat started after midnight. As soon as we got out of range of the Brussels street lamps the chauffeur's courage failed. As we passed through a small wood he saw bandits and devils in every tree. His wife filled the air with lamentable cries of terror, in which the two dogs joined. I first encouraged, then threatened the driver, but his fears were such that he gave all his mind to arguing about bandits and devils, and constantly ran off the road. At each of these stoppages he pleaded that we might wait for the morning. Finally I enlisted the help of a Civic Guard who reassured him that no bandits nor devils were in front, whilst I told him lurid stories of Uhlans behind. His wife began to take my view, and I think I heard her in Flemish advise him to obey.

On reaching a place of safety for the motor, about fifteen kilometres out of Brussels, I awaited the morning. As soon as it was dawn the chauffeur insisted on returning to Brussels. My luggage was turned out by the roadside, and he went off, whilst I mounted a bicycle to return to Brussels, hoping fervently that the Uhlans would take him, his wife, and their dogs and-treat them very kindly.

From Brussels I went out on the road towards Louvain until I came into touch with the German advance posts marching into the city. Then I turned back to Brussels and waited there until after the departure of the last officials and made for the Dutch frontier with no impedimenta but a cycle.

As I left Brussels there were no signs remaining of the panic overnight. Except that the city was stripped of its guards and that the railway services had ceased all was normal.

The markets were open and great stocks of fruit and vegetables exposed for sale. The citizens who had remained (a great majority) were preparing to make the best of things. Refugees were still arriving from Louvain, but nothing untoward had happened there, and one family I met announced its intention of going back to Louvain; but most of the fugitives passed through Brussels towards the coast or remained in the capital.

Brussels fell on August 20th. Namur fell three days later after a resistance the briefness of which excited much adverse comment. I was not within the Namur area during the attack on the fortress (after the fall of Brussels I went to Antwerp, via Holland), and so have no direct knowledge of the events, but I saw subsequently several of the officers concerned in the defence, and they claimed that the short resistance of Namur as compared with Liége was due not to any failure on the part of the Namur garrison and the field Army, but to the simple fact that the Germans attacked Liége without specially heavy artillery, but Namur with guns of great calibre.

At Liége for the first two days the Germans bombarded the forts with field artillery and howitzer batteries, at the same time attacking the intervals between the forts. The result was a heavy German loss. Taught a lesson by this, the Germans made no field army attack on the intervals between the forts at Namur. They stood far away with guns of twenty-eight centimetres calibre, and with an extensive bombardment prepared the way for the infantry advance. The forts of Maizeret and De Marchovolette were converted into ruins. The forts of Cognelee and Andoy were also put out of action with all the entrenchments between them. Thus fully half of the circle of forts were swept away before a German infantry advance was attempted. It was a victory for guns such as had never been brought into the field before.

The Belgian field Force made a good resistance. But because of the great numerical superiority of the Germans within the sections assailed and because of the superior force of their batteries, which could now take in the rear the remaining

Namur forts, the contest was hopeless. On the 23rd August the retreat was ordered at midday. If it had been delayed another twelve hours, retreat would have been impossible.

To show the intensity of the bombardment, the commandant of the fort of Maizeret got an officer to count the shells of the enemy falling within the fort. They numbered two thousand per day during two and a half days.

An "official explanation" of the fall of Namur was issued by the Belgian Ministry for War on September 13th. It stated:

"According to information received at the Ministry of War, and which is confirmed by the report of Lieutenant-General Michel, commanding the 4th Division of our army, the fortified position of Namur suffered a continuous bombardment during three days and two nights. A tremendous quantity of projectiles were used, not only against the forts but also against the spaces between the forts. The German Artillery employed cannon of 5, 10, 13, 15, 21 and 28 centimetres. It was the enormous 28-centimetre guns which destroyed the defences. The fire was so continuous that it was impossible to attempt to repair the damage done between the forts. The fort of Suarlee, for instance, was bombarded from Sunday morning, the 23rd of August, and fell on the 25th at 5 o'clock in the afternoon. Three German batteries of large cannon, using projectiles weighing 350 kilos, shot 600 projectiles on the 23rd, 1,300 on the 24th, and about 1,400 on the 25th against this fort. When the fort fell, all the massive central structure was destroyed and further resistance was hopeless.

"These few facts enable us to assert that the fall of the forts of Namur and the retreat of the 4th Division can be perfectly explained without accusing the garrison of insufficient resistance."

At Antwerp in September, I chatted with a number of survivors of the Namur field Defence Force [the Fourth Division), and they told me the story of the defence. It was full of vivid interest. After repulsing the Germans at Warthez on August 22nd, this Belgian division found itself compelled to fight an action of retreat against an overwhelming force, of which the most dangerous element was the heavy artillery. On August 23rd they were just in front of Namur, with the Germans apparently all round. They were almost without officers owing to the heavy losses in the preceding battles. The resolution was made to attempt to break through the German lines – at a gap to the south-west along a line passing east of Philippeville. By night this was successfully accomplished, horse, foot and artillery gliding through under the very nose of the enemy, taking elaborate precautions to smother the sound of wheels and of horses.

At dawn on the 24th, the Belgian Division had got to the French lines at Biouh Rosee and Mariembourg. But the general falling back was then in progress, and it was impossible to rest for more than a few hours. The Belgians retired with the French to Couvin, then to Auvilliers. They were offered there the option of joining with the French forces or going back to the main Belgian Army by sea. They chose the latter, and travelled by Rouen and Zeebrugge.

A young University student of the force told me how at Rouen the men, wearied in spirit by the trials through which they had passed, were inspired with fresh courage by an old priest. This priest, who had fought in the war of 1870, has a little church at Petit Couronne (which was Corneille's village, just outside Rouen). On August 28th, when the Belgian soldiers arrived, the Abbé assembled them in the forest, and at a drumhead altar conducted Divine Service to music by the band of the 10th Regiment, which, having lost its own instruments in the retreat, used others borrowed in the village. The men recall now with tears in their eyes that solemn service in the wood and the sermon of Abbé Lemire. They say that such an ardent flame of patriotism and courage burned in his eyes and lifted his voice from out the feebleness of old age, making it ring like a clarion, that their souls were lifted up and their spirit renewed.

With Liége, Louvain, Brussels and Namur in the hands of the enemy, the Belgian Army now rallied at Antwerp.

CHAPTER V

AFTER the Belgian Army had broken at Tirlemont there was no attempt at an enterprising pursuit on the part of the Germans. The retreating Belgian forces reached the Antwerp fortress without serious loss other than that suffered on the battlefield, and at once the Belgian King and his Government set about the task of their reorganization, setting aside without hesitation the renewed invitations to an armistice which came from the German Emperor.

I did not follow the Belgian Army on its retreat from Tirlemont and Louvain farther than Malines, for I then turned back to Brussels to watch the fate of that city. I reached Antwerp via Holland on the night of Saturday, August 22nd, and the next day, renewing my relations with the Belgian Army, saw that its leaders were facing the situation resolute and undismayed. The city was saddened a little, but calm and courageous, and I found a new cause for acclaiming the Belgians in the dignified fortitude with which they bore the misfortune imposed upon them by the war tactics of Europe's enemy.

In Amsterdam the previous day I had been informed with impressive circumstantial evidence that the whole Belgian population was panic-stricken, that Antwerp was surrounded by Germans, cut off from all communications, that the Royal Family was preparing to flee, that the unfortunate city had no supplies of food, and finally, for my special benefit, that a proclamation of the Minister for War stated that foreign journalists found on Belgian soil would be shot. All this came from Hollanders who professed to be antagonistic to Germany and sympathetic to Belgium. They told these facts with tears in their eyes, and nothing appeared to give them more sorrow than the thought of the despair of Belgium.

I was convinced that the German Secret Service, recognizing the hopelessness of getting news accepted from Berlin, was using Holland as a base for circulating its falsehoods, for all I was told about Antwerp and most of what I was told about the war was "pro-German" falsehood.

I got through to Antwerp quite easily, though slowly (far more slowly on the Dutch side than the Belgian side). On the way I encountered Antwerp business men making a trip to London, and intending to return next Tuesday. At the Customs a bicycle, which since my flight from Brussels represented all my baggage, was passed without duty, and I had a glad welcome at the War Office and Staff headquarters. I walked through the city without challenge, seeing everywhere the normal life. True, the *cafés* were less crowded, the churches more crowded than usual, but there was not a sign that the brave Belgians were dismayed, though many signs that they recognized the importance of the task which had fallen on them as the vanguard of Europe.

Some signs of seriousness were that the places of amusement were closed, the *cafés* had to shut their doors at ten, and spirits might not be sold, though wine and beer were still allowed.

Regarding events outside of Antwerp, I learned that the mass of the German Army was moving south from Brussels: that some bands of Uhlans had gone in the direction of Ghent, but that it was hoped to clear these away. News from Brussels stated that on Friday after I had left the authorities cleared the roads of barbed wire and the streets of all impediments, including the *café* tables and chairs, and most of the *cafés* closed their doors.

The Civic Guards were disarmed, and the authorities made energetic appeals to the citizens to refrain from any demonstrations. There were some painful scenes when it was explained to the Boy Scouts that the Germans would not recognize their uniforms, and that they must return to civil attire. The Scouts, who had done noble work as Red Cross helpers, couriers, guides, and, indeed, as courteous friends to all in trouble, pleaded that they should be allowed to keep their uniform and continue their duties. Said one: "We have our duty to accomplish. Have we not still the right to help the wounded and suffering?" But the German orders were inexorable. "No more Boy Scouts in Brussels."

At the last moment the United States Minister took his place by the side of the Brussels Burgomaster, M. Max, and informed the German officers that he had a mission from the American

Government to take the city under his protection and see that the laws of war were respected. In the afternoon German officers proceeded in motor-cars to the town hall, and other detachments of German troops crossed the town at various points. The railway stations were closed. The town kept calm, and the only signs of animation were caused by the unceasing influx of fugitives into the city. These were not interfered with, but no one was allowed to leave.

Life in Antwerp on Monday, August 24th, was almost cheerful. The citizens took a keen delight in the presence among them of the King and Queen, and the royal children. It was generally anticipated that, since the German Army had been delayed from August 3rd to August 24th, a full three weeks, in Belgium, it would on reaching the French frontier find the French and British Armies well prepared to meet it, would soon be rolled back and that the liberation of Belgium would speedily follow.

But the next day a shadow of tragedy came over the city and it deepened daily until the last hours of bombardment and surrender. Early on the morning of August 25th, the Germans committed a murderous outrage on the population of Antwerp, so gross as to be almost inconceivable, at that stage of the war. (Since we have known our Hun better.) At one in the morning I was aroused by the sound of a heavy explosion, which shook the room in which I was sleeping. I rushed into the street, heard five more great explosions, and saw a Zeppelin hovering over the west of the city. It disappeared, followed by ineffectual rifle fire from the Civic Guard.

By following the civic authorities from place to place, I obtained the facts regarding a horrible feat of midnight assassination. It was clear that the soldiers of the German Emperor had chiefly designed the murder of the Belgian Royal Family. Stealing silently over the forts outside the city, against which no attack was made, the Zeppelin steered towards the temporary Royal Palace and discharged a number of high-explosive bombs. Not one found its mark exactly. All fell close within the precincts of the Palace. One narrowly escaped the tower of Antwerp Cathedral, and three found human victims. The most successful struck a private house inhabited by poor people, murdered a pregnant woman, and horribly mutilated three young girls, killed two

Civic Guards, and seriously injured another. The second bomb, falling in the street, killed one and wounded two. Another bomb, falling into the courtyard of the Hospital of St.Elisabeth, tore a great hole in the ground, smashed the windows, riddled the walls with the fragments, but killed no one, though a crucifix over the bed of a sick child was smashed to pieces. In all I heard of seven killed and five wounded that night.

It was at a private house just off the Place de Meir that the first bomb fell. It tore up the top storey and split up the front. As I arrived a woman tottered out covered with lime dust, crying out "Docteur, docteur." Beneath the ruins of the house two Civic Guards were dead. Within the house pitiful screams came from three girls, who had been aroused from sleep by receiving dreadful wounds on the face and body. One girl had half her face blown away, the two others were seriously wounded on the face. Evidently their bodies had been somewhat protected by the bed-clothes.

I recovered pieces of one of the Zeppelin shells which showed that it had been very large, with thick walls filled with a high explosive. Later in the morning I made exhaustive investigations directed towards the finding of some other explanation than a German attempt on the Palace.

Was it possible, for example, that seeing the Zeppelin over the city, the forts fired upon her and the shells fell within the town? That explanation had to be rejected. The shells were big, high-explosive ones and had fallen directly from above within a limited area. Every bomb told the same story: that which destroyed the house, that which ravaged the Hospital, that which fell in the Rue des Escrimeurs, those which fell on the other streets. They were not fired from any gun, and they all indicated the trail of the Zeppelin passing from east to west, aiming at the Palace, and ravaging its neighbourhood.

Later investigation showed that ten persons were killed and eight wounded by the Zeppelin bombs. All were of the civil population, and more than a third were women. A reconstruction of the bombs showed them to have been ten inches in diameter, the envelope being nearly an inch thick. They were loaded with picrite. The airship must have drifted down the wind without using its propellers, for no sound was heard until it was over the city. In the direction of its bombs it was probably helped by local spies.

Among the residents of Antwerp at the time was Surgeon-Major Seaman of the reserve of the Army Medical Corps of the United States.

During August 25th he was in attendance on some of the Zeppelin wounded. He made a statement to me that in all his eight campaigns, of which one was against the Boxers in China, he had never seen an incident of war so ruthless, so horrible, as the sight of three young girls mutilated and defaced, and of a dead young mother, all attacked in their beds at night. So inflamed was he that he demanded that the United States should at once join in exacting reparation from Germany for such infamies. I assisted Major Seaman to communicate his views to a representative New York paper, and clearly it was valuable in arousing public opinion in America against such atrocities. Almost every New York paper made Major Seaman's message the text for an indignant article. Some examples:

The *New York Times:* "The dropping of bombs into the city of Antwerp from a German Zeppelin airship is a crime against humanity of which civilized nations should take notice by earnest protests to the German Government. By dropping bombs upon the city the persons in control of the Zeppelin showed that they were willing to take innocent human lives, lives of men, women and children alike, in sheer wantonness, for the killing of inhabitants of Antwerp by this means can be of no possible advantage to the armies of Germany and has no rational place in her war plans."

The *New York Sun:* "To murder wantonly and pitilessly, to slay or mangle little children and young mothers in their beds, to salute the Red Cross flag with a bomb, and to slaughter and terrorize non-combatants; random destruction, with no military results, with no permanent result except to sicken and anger all civilized mankind - this is war as practised on the city from Zeppelin airships. Every nation which still believes that something of humanity should be maintained in the usages of warfare should raise its voice against this arch-deed of pitiless savagery, against a repetition of such senseless and unforgivable blind massacre."

The *New York World:* "If the accounts of this Zeppelin exploit are true this was downright murder which cannot be excused by any exigencies of war."

The *New York Tribune:* "It is a wanton act of destruction."

The *New York Herald:* "Official defenders of Germany may feel called upon to furnish some defence of the employment of what the world is very likely to characterize as inhuman and barbarous methods."

The *Washington Post:* "The civilized world will never condone the slaying of innocent civilians in their own homes by means of bombs dropped from a balloon. This is not war, but mere ruthless butchery. No military necessity requires a balloon to sail over the dwellings of civilians and destroy their occupants."

The *Washington Times:* "An effort to terrorize a city outside the war zone by dropping bombs where they could only destroy the property and menace the lives of non-combatants is barbarism in the last degree."

The United States Government, however, as an indication of its "neutrality" threatened to strike the courageous Major Seaman's name off its Army List because he had referred to the German Zeppelin as coming on its murderous mission "like a hyena in the night." That was, however, no more than the truth picturesquely expressed. If the Zeppelin bombs had been directed at the forts no one could have complained; but the airship, sneaking past the forts, deliberately bombarded the civil quarters of the town some five miles distant.

The effect of this Zeppelin outrage on the citizens of Antwerp was profoundly disquieting, though they did not allow it to intimidate them. They could see now the extent to which German ruthlessness was prepared to go and connected the bomb-dropping (probably correctly) with the rage of the Germans at the latest refusal on the part of Belgium to play the traitor. "The man in the street" could tell me, with circumstantial detail, that the German Emperor had threatened to treat the Belgian King, if he did not yield, as a "personal enemy" and had decreed his assassination.

As a means of precaution against further Zeppelin visits it was decreed that the lights of Antwerp should be put out at 8 p.m. and the darkness of the city affected profoundly the citizens, who had been accustomed during the summer nights to promenade the boulevards or to sit on the terraces of the *cafés* until midnight and after.

The first night of darkness was unforgettable. Antwerp spent that night in anticipation of another Zeppelin raid, but the murderous work of the previous night was not repeated. At eight o'clock all lights were extinguished in the city, the *cafés* were closed and the trams stopped.

Motors, carriages and cycles had to proceed without lights except in special cases. I made a tour of the city at ten o'clock. It was a clear, still night, and the stars gave just enough light to distinguish strong outlines. The streets were dark caverns, showing a few masked lights for the use of the military hospitals. From private houses no lights were shown. Civilization, on guard against barbarism, took refuge in darkness. Some proportion of the civil population stumbled aimlessly along through the dark streets; the greater proportion assembled outside their houses and watched the skies fearfully. Now and again a woman's hysterical cry heralded falsely the dreaded monster in the sky. Some never sought their couches during the whole night. They would have been safer within doors, but they had that curious human instinct to meet death, if it were to come, standing up. In darkness and dread Antwerp awaited the dawn. One incident of the night was the removal at the Central Station of two trainloads of wounded arrived from Malines. The work had to be carried on in absolute darkness.

On August 30th I recorded my impressions of the previous week at Antwerp:

"Evening Service in the great Cathedral of Antwerp: the devout-war has recruited their ranks, the Zeppelin outrage has sent their eyes in hope as well as in fear towards Heaven- fill the nave. The gorgeously-robed statue of Our Lady of Intercession is hedged around with thickets of burning tapers The *Anversois* come these days often to their churches with candles, which they light as if to say to Heaven: 'Deign to look down upon us here. True, we have sought the good things of the world, but out of our riches to Thee we have raised great fanes, and richly decked them. Regard us now and have mercy.'

"Vespers have been sung and a sermon Flemish preached-a sermon of encouragement and patriotism.
It is the time for *Le Salut*, the service which English Catholics know as 'Benediction'. Choir and organ burst into the hymn of and hope:

> *O Salutaris Hostia,*
> *Quæ Cœli pandis ostium.*
> *Bella premunt hostilia,*
> *Da robur, fer auxilium.*

"A movement, a rustling goes through the whole congregation. It is as if everyone took a deep breath and then sighed. With all their souls these *Anversois* join in the cry for strength, for help.

"A little later a Litany is chanted, and the mass of the people, joining in the Responses, send echoing under the Gothic roof cries which sound as the rolling of drums.

*   *   *   *   *

"A woman, mother of four little children living next door to a house where three were killed by the Zeppelin bombs, speaks to me of it the next day. Her wan face is worn with the terrors of the night and the fears of the future. But she summons up a pitiful smile for the Englishman. 'Ah, sir, it is not gay, this war,' she says bravely.

*   *   *   *   *

"A little fatherless boy, holding to his mother's skirts (refugees from a village near Malines), wide-eyed, solemn, but apparently not terrified, says to a questioner: 'When I am a man I shall kill all the Germans.'
With a quick gesture-was it of dread of a German over-

54

heating, or compunction that her child should speak so? – his mother put a hand over his mouth. The boy then was silent, but his fixed, solemn eyes told that his thoughts were still terrible.

*   *   *   *   *

"The garden of an *estaminet*, near Duffel, through which the stream of refugees from Louvain and Malines passes. Every room is crowded with sleeping peasants, some of whom had walked all through a night and a day in flight before the German hordes. Those seeking for shelter have overflowed into the garden. Thirty or more are sleeping there, the sleep of utter fatigue. A very old woman has a mattress under a tree. A son of perhaps eighteen shelters his mother's head in his lap and sleeps, himself sitting, his back propped against a tree. On the face of a young woman there are ineradicable traces of a great horror. Her features are convulsed now and again as she sleeps.

*   *   *   *   *

"In the Cathedral Church of Antwerp, as I pass, the people are assembling for a solemn Mass of Requiem for the late Pope. I go out towards Malines (whose Cardinal Bishop was expected by many to be the next Pope) and see his Cathedral under the bombs of the German guns fired in purely destructive savagery against a town without forts and without troops.

*   *   *   *   *

"That war could be so savage; that human beings under such horrors could be so patient and courageous as the Belgians are patient and courageous, I would never have believed had I not passed through these days of the agony of Belgium."

Early on the morning of September 2nd, the Zeppelin assassins visited Antwerp again, but failed to kill anyone, though three persons were wounded by its bombs. The precautions taken by the Belgian authorities proved fairly efficacious, for the Zeppelin was attacked from the forts and the high points of the city as soon as it made its appearance, and the absence of any lights in the city clearly puzzled the raiders.

The net result was that the Zeppelin suddenly dropped all its bombs in a panic over the poor quarter of the city and disappeared, having effected little damage.

I was aroused at half-past three by the sound of rifle and cannon firing, and rushed into the street. I just caught a glimpse of the Zeppelin which had passed over the city, hurrying away and rising rapidly.

It was under heavy fire from rifles, Maxims and field pieces. From the sky near the tower I saw a great flashlight and thought at first it was a bomb which had been discharged by a gun from the Zeppelin, but later it was clear that it was a shell discharged at the Zeppelin. Later came the sound of one great explosion, which seemed to be discharged from a naval gun. Running around various points of the city from which the fusillade was still kept up, though the airship had disappeared, I was assured that no damage had been done and that the Zeppelin had discharged no bomb.

But closer investigation showed that what for the discharge of a great gun was really the sound of the explosion, almost simultaneously, of about nine bombs from the Zeppelin. Apparently the airship had been unable to repeat its stab in the dark, and failing to find its bearings in the darkened city, had become alarmed when under fire, and had dropped suddenly all its bombs as a means of rising quickly. The bombs found their mark in a poor quarter, where the city's refuse is spread out for rag-pickers to sort. One fell in an unsavoury field, tearing a hole in the ground nine feet in diameter and five feet deep. Another tore the back out of a house a few yards away. Another smashed a poor hut. Several fell into an unoccupied house to which is attached a diamond-cutter's workrooms and smashed it and the neighbouring house. Three people were seriously, seven people slightly injured by the fragments of the shell and *débris*. One man I saw had his face scratched all over as if by an angry cat.

In most cases the wounds were slight; the most seriously injured was a young girl. Such was the notable victory for the Germans on the anniversary of Sedan.

I talked with some of the dwellers in the neighbourhood attacked. One was an old woman whose husband was a paralytic. A bomb entered their poor house, tore down the attic in which they slept, and cast them on the ground of the floor uninjured. The paralysed man could not move, and his wife would not flee without him. They waited for morning, hand in hand. Another woman was sleeping in bed with two daughters. The second storey of the villa was thrown down through the destroyed floors into the cellar. The inmates were only bruised slightly.

It is clear that the place of discharge was accidental rather than deliberate. Further, the shells on this occasion were not of the same type of high explosive designed to destroy *matériel*, but were a fiendish variety of shrapnel of immense size loaded with a great quantity of iron bolts and nuts designed most evidently for the destruction of human life. They were, in fact, anarchist bombs on a large scale. Aided with fragments representing almost all of one shell I was able to assure myself absolutely that this time the Zeppelin's cargo would have been almost useless against *matériel*, but of awful power of slaughter in a crowded quarter.

Naturally the population of Antwerp was deeply moved. But, accepting the wise advice of the authorities, few came out into the streets. Most of the inhabitants who were aroused took to their cellars, not to the streets. The city the next day was reassured rather than terrified, for it was seen that the precautions of the authorities had prevented the loss of human life on this occasion.

As the result of investigating these two and other Zeppelin attempts, some observations regarding this form of attack may be useful for other cities. It would seem that the carrying power of Zeppelins has been grossly exaggerated. It may be accepted that the Germans did their worst possible in the two attacks on Antwerp. The results achieved, whilst shocking to civilization, were not such as to be intimidating to a belligerent. It seemed clear that proper precautions could guard almost wholly against airships with such powers of mischief as had been demonstrated up to then. The Antwerp precautions against Zeppelins generally took two main lines, to mask the city by extinguishing almost all the lights, and to establish searchlights, sharpshooters, and Maxims on high points around the city. The dread inspired by the Zeppelin is, of course, great, but probably the nervousness of the people below is much less than the nervousness of the people above in an airship when finding themselves under observation and under fire.

The courage of King Albert and his Consort Queen Elisabeth during these days in Antwerp was notable.

After the first Zeppelin attack, since it was clear that the Royal Family had been specially aimed at by the German bomb-throwers, advice was given to the King to retire with his family from Antwerp. He refused sturdily. The Queen left for England to take her children to a place of safety and then promptly returned to her husband's side and followed him through all the dark days of September, October and November.

The same courage filled the army and the nation. The day of the first Zeppelin outrage the army moved out by Fort Waelhem and inflicted a heavy defeat on the Germans at Malines. It was no mere skirmish. The Germans were driven back with horse, foot and artillery. The cathedral at Malines suffered somewhat from the German shells (clearly directed specially at it), but the town was not much injured on this occasion. The combat at dawn, when the Belgian forces moved from Malines and attacked a German force had advanced from the south during previous three days, and which with its patrols had been attacking the environs of Malines. The German position was along the line of the canal to Louvain. In artillery work the Belgians showed superiority. Pushing forward their infantry drove back the Germans once with a bayonet charge.

For this enterprise the Germans inflicted a barbarous penalty. They now made up their minds to give a really drastic lesson to this heroic little people who had proved so méchant in defending themselves when attacked. The horrors of Louvain followed hard upon the sally of the Belgian Army.

CHAPTER VI

LOUVAIN: GERMAN FRIGHTFULNESS

IT was only after the occupation of Brussels and the continued refusal of the Belgian people to give way and allow the German path through their country to be undisturbed that the era of organized atrocities began. These atrocities were part of a deliberate policy of an attempt to conquer a nation through the tears of its women and the blood of its little children when military measures had proved not sufficient to subdue its spirit.

Translate into the terms of civil life the campaign in Belgium, and it would read like this: Carl Schmidt, having the desire to attack Henri Dubois, asks the mutual friend and neighbour of both, little Jean Vendele, to help him. Jean refuses.

"Very well then," says Carl, "I shall beat you to a pulp."

"Even so," replies Jean, "I refuse to help you to kill our neighbour." Carl, enraged, considers this an unreasonable attitude and proceeds to attempt to coerce Jean by burning his house, killing his children, violating his wife and defiling the altars at which Jean worships.

When the time comes for Germany to pay the reckoning of her monstrous passage across Belgium it will be useless to put forward the plea that the acts of atrocity which now cry to Heaven for vengeance were due to the vile passions of individual soldiers. The German campaign of outrage and brutality in Belgium was deliberate, organized, foreseen, provided for with scientific machinery. Let that sentence have a reservation that the words "In Belgium" may not stand on final investigation.

Possibly the preparations were for England, and it was hoped before the war that Belgium would sell the pass and that a fortnight after war was declared the triumphant German Army would be ranged from Havre to Antwerp, with its special outrage machinery, waiting the chance to descend on Great Britain. But whether for England, for Belgium, or for France, the campaign of outrage was part of the planned method of the German rulers.

Many facts prove this. Special machinery for incendiarism

accompanied the German forces; special drill for it had been taught; the Germans burned out a town with the methodical correctness with which a German battery went into action. Again, a town was usually as a response to a German defeat, and in one case, at least, the sack of an undefended town was threatened as a blackmailing attempt to secure the surrender of a for some miles distant. So far I have not been able to secure positive verification of the commonly-reported, commonly-believed statement that as a last attempt to bully Belgium into an act of treachery the German Emperor telegraphed to King Albert of Belgium a threat to treat him as a "personal enemy" and to "sack" Belgium. Only the King can speak on that point, and as yet he is silent.

But many circumstances suggest the truth of the statement. Belgium has been "sacked" in large part, and personal attempts on the King's life - not alone by Zeppelin bombs - have been be impressed on the mind of civilized Europe that the agony which endured has not been due in the first instance to sudden and unexpected brutality on the part of soldiers in the field. It is the result of the policy of the Emperor, the policy of Germany. That the "policy" of outrage was carried in some instances farther than was intended may be allowed. That was due to tendencies but little flattering to our common human nature. The German Army, trained beforehand for rapine, destruction, and murder, responded ignobly to the call to the brute in man, and soon learned to add torture to murder and strange degenerate acts of sacrilege and mad nastiness to destruction. Officers and soldiers were not always content to kill out of hand and to burn quickly. They had to torture beforehand, and to desecrate and insult beautiful buildings before destroying them.

A Belgian friend, talking on the point, used the illustration (from a Fourain cartoon) of a low-minded servant, in envy of her beautiful mistress, deliberately soiling the pillow on which she would sleep. It is exact. Beautiful churches, carved out – nay, rather stitched – in lace-like stone by medieval piety, have been befouled. In one chateau of rare beauty the German officers, after pillaging the cellar and destroying the marbles and bronzes, brought in a cow from the fields, disembowelled it, and spread its entrails and blood over the carpets-and tapestries!

Very frequently torture was applied to the peasants-physical and moral torture of the cruellest kind.

Peasants have been kept on their knees with hands uplifted for hours under threat of instant death if they moved. They been shut up and told to be ready to die in three hours; then released, then shut up again, and sentenced to death. They have been shut up for long periods with hardly any food or water, and with no means to observe the decencies of life. Sometimes death has followed torture of this kind, sometimes not. I have told to me scores of stories of torture by sufferers who showed but too plainly the truth of what they said; and the many mad people (mostly women) encountered-driven made by German brutality-told more plainly than by coherent speech what they had suffered.

Plainly, our human nature shelters still much of the tiger and the ape, ready to show out monstrous when the barriers of law and civilization are swept away by criminals in high places. Some of the German officers and men have been exceptions to the rule, and have shown pity to the people they have wronged, But too many have been ready to respond to the call for brutality and foul outrage made by their Emperor. There is cogent reason why Europe should take precaution that such a call does not come again.

In a consideration of the German atrocities in Belgium, it is more important to seek out the causes than to concentrate attention on the details. I shall not attempt to catalogue the full sickening list of horrors (those who have the strength to do so can read the details in the official reports), but will refer to a few of the more characteristic crimes which came under my direct notice.

The sack of Louvain was the chief of these. I was in Malines on Thursday, August 27th.

The Germans were shelling the town (or rather its cathedral, for the gun-fire seemed exclusively directed on to the Cathedral square) at noon when there came flowing into the city a stream of refugees from Louvain with such tales of horror as, hearing, rebuked sleep and made all the comforts of life seem odious to me for many days after.

Returning to Antwerp, I was the first to inform the Belgian

officials there of what had happened at Louvain. My statement was received at first with incredulity, but was soon confirmed by official inquiry. That night I telegraphed to the *Morning Post* a brief account. It was held back by the British authorities for day as it seemed an unbelievable horror; and afterwards published. These facts I record because they show that my account was absolutely independent of all Belgian prompting (being actually the first to reach Antwerp or London). Though brief and inadequate, I will reproduce that report now as it was written so that it may be compared with the official account. Some slight inaccuracies, some material omissions I leave uncorrected. It will be seen that in the main facts the Belgian official account and my account agree. There will be a German official account of the crime of Louvain-some indications of it have been already given-and a necessary part of that German official account will be to attempt to argue that the Belgian Government "trumped up" the Louvain accusation, seeking to misrepresent a stern act of war into a case of horrible, causeless outrage. I trust that my account* will be of some value as the evidence of an unprejudiced witness.

On August 27th I telegraphed:

"Louvain was sacked on Wednesday night by the Germans. A great part of the population was massacred, including women, children and clergy. Their nationality did not save English and American clergymen. All the noble public buildings, including the town hall [this was incorrect], the library, and the University, were destroyed. That is the tale of horror disclosed at Malines by fleeing refugees. It is confirmed by the Procureur and by escaped notables from the destroyed city. The atrocity seems incredible, but there is no reason to doubt its truth. "What was the cause of this sudden outbreak of the German spirit in its full atrociousness one cannot as yet say. The refugees can tell only of the horrors; they can give no reason. But what seems to have happened is that the German Army, defeated at Malines the previous day, fell back on Louvain in some disorder, reaching the town in the evening.

*Up to the date of the Zeppelin raid on Antwerp, August 25th, 1914, I had not accepted a single accusation of atrocity against the Germans, and on one occasion, August 16th, had put on record my conclusion that there was up to then no proof of atrocities.

German fugitives were fired upon in error by their own troops. Rage at this misfortune and chagrin over defeat seem to have inflamed the rage of the barbarians, who set to work systematically to massacre the population and to destroy the city, whose monuments belonged as much to civilization as to Belgium.

"It is not possible to put upon paper the accounts of the fugitives. They were given in gestures, in broken exclamations, rather than in sentences. The purport was always the same, that the civil population had done nothing, but that last night, when retreating German soldiers began to arrive, suddenly the Germans became angry and began to slaughter, pillage and destroy. None of the horrors of the worst incidents of barbarian warfare seem to have been lacking. These Huns of the Twentieth Century gave full rein to cruelty, lust, and a fiendish spirit of destruction, sparing neither women children nor ministers of religion, nor the beautiful monuments of medieval piety. From what was told to me nothing remains of Louvain but ruins, nor of its population but fugitives.

"It is possible that when the full story comes to be told it will be found that the horror is not quite so great, for all the accounts are from people fleeing for their lives; but among those people were four civic dignitaries who were in the city during the night, and who were actually in the hands of the Germans, but escaped. Their relation of the facts is what is followed in this despatch, for it is more likely to be accurate and sober. They are inclined to think that it was German rage at the defeat of Malines which set aflame the barbarian passions. They declared emphatically that since the unopposed occupation of Louvain by the Germans a week ago the civil population had given no cause of offence.

The attack upon the unarmed population came suddenly, the Germans firing in the streets, going from house to house, pillaging, ravishing, murdering and setting houses on fire. Neither age nor sex was respected. Almost all the clergy were shot" [this was an exaggeration: though many were], "including one English and one American clergyman. The monstrous work continued through the night. In the morning those officials who had taken refuge in a church were driven out of the town at the point of the bayonet, and not killed. The fit of murderous rage had evidently passed.

"On the road from Louvain to Antwerp crowds of pitiful refugees could be seen-nuns fleeing from their cloisters, priests from their churches, the sick carried on their beds, the aged tottering along with the help of their children, all who could carrying some poor article of household furniture. In one cart were collected seventeen children, evidently of several families. Another hand-cart held an old, palsied woman, pushed on by her grandchild. All were fleeing from the Huns and poured into Antwerp as a city of refuge-a city which now shudders in darkness through the nights at the fear of midnight bombs.

Among the train of fugitives were ambulances of the Belgian Army, in which were carried solicitously the German wounded to the hospitals.

On August 28th I telegraphed:

"The exact extent of the German atrocities at Louvain cannot yet be stated. I spent this morning at Duffel, Contich, and near Malines interviewing refugees from Louvain. All have the same story of great horror, but it varies in detail. All agree that a great part of the town has been burned; it is in regard to the extent of the massacre that there is disagreement. Two peasants who had come from the city on foot said it was all in flames, and that the Germans had driven the whole population out of the town at the point of the bayonet, forcing them to march with their hands up for over an hour. These peasants said nothing about a general massacre.

"A peasant woman said her husband had been killed, and all the men killed. Another peasant said that people were burned in their homes, and another that the Germans had taken all the young women, driving others out of the town.

"I made the best effort possible to penetrate through to Louvain or its vicinity. The Belgian General gave me a safe conduct for the Belgian lines, but his officers were urgent in warnings as to the extreme danger of going forward. I got to a point east of Malines. I then found it absolutely hopeless to go further, for I was beyond the last Belgian outpost. The countryside was deserted of all peasants, and German vedette outposts were in every direction. With a friendly peasant it would perhaps have been possible to follow by-roads and get to Louvain, but all the peasants had fled before the barbarians.

"Reluctantly I turned back, and was a little consoled to encounter M. Eugene Paquet, a business man of substance and integrity, who had from a friend of his who lived at Louvain, and had fled from there when the sack had gone on some time, a direct account of the night's horror. This friend has a high official position, that of Inspector of Public Works in the province. I understood he could not be directly interviewed today, because the horrors and hardships of the night had prostrated him, but his story as repeated to me by M. Paquet confirms the facts which I telegraphed last night.

"The origin of the atrocity was German resentment over the Belgian victory at Malines. The inhabitants were ordered out into the streets and volleys fired into them. Then men and women were separated on different sides of the street and the men were driven forward out of the town at the point of the bayonet, many being killed. The chief public buildings, not including the Town Hall, were set on fire and wrecked with explosives.

"News which comes from Malines today suggests that this monstrous horror at Louvain was not the result of the mad rage of an isolated body of soldiers, but is part of the deliberate German plan to fight the Belgian Army with the weapons of massacre and destruction of civil property, so as to immobilize it without too great an expense of German soldiery. Today the Burgomaster of Malines came in to Brussels with news that the German commander had demanded the surrender of the outermost of the Antwerp forts, or else Malines would be razed to the ground. So far the barbarians have spared Malines.

"When I visited the town yesterday under the nose of the German scouts, the Cathedral was only slightly damaged. Two shells had struck the tower, five had pierced the roof, one had pierced a window, and some other slight damage had been done."

The Belgian official account of the sack of Louvain, communicated to the public on September 15th, but dated August 31st, reads:

"At nightfall on August 26th the German troops, repulsed by our soldiers, entered Louvain panic-struck. Several witnesses affirm that the German garrison which occupied Louvain was erroneously informed that the enemy were entering the town. Men of the garrison immediately marched to the station, shooting hap-hazard the while, and there met the German troops who had been repulsed by the Belgians, the latter having just ceased the pursuit.

Everything tends to prove that the German regiments fired on one another. At once the Germans began bombarding the town, pretending that civilians had fired on the troops, a suggestion which is contradicted by all the witnesses, and could scarcely have been possible, because the inhabitants of Louvain had had to give up their arms to the municipal authorities several days before. The bombardment lasted till about ten o'clock at night. The Germans then set fire to the town. Wherever the fire had not spread the German soldiers entered the houses and threw fire grenades, with which some of them seem to be provided. The greater part of the town of Louvain was thus a prey to the flames, particularly the quarters of the upper town, comprising the modern buildings, the ancient Cathedral of St. Pierre, the University Buildings, together with the University Library, its manuscripts and collections, and the Municipal Theatre.

"The Commission considers it its duty to insist, in the midst of all these horrors, on the crime committed against civilization by the deliberate destruction of an academic library which was one of the treasures of Europe.

"The corpses of many civilians encumbered the streets and squares. On the road from Tirlemont to Louvain alone a witness counted more than fifty. On the doorsteps of houses could be seen carbonized bodies of inhabitants, who, hiding in their cellars, were driven out by the fire, tried to escape, and fell into the flames.

The suburbs of Louvain suffered the same fate. We can affirm that the houses in all the districts between Louvain and Malines and most of the suburbs of Louvain itself have practically been destroyed.

"On Wednesday morning, 26th August, the Germans brought to the Station Square of Louvain a group of more than seventy-five persons, including several prominent citizens of the town, amongst whom were Father Coloboet and another Spanish priest, and also an American priest. The men were brutally separated from their wives and children, and after having been subject to the most abominable treatment by the Germans, who several times threatened to shoot them, they were forced to march to the village of Campenhout in front of the German troops. They were shut up in the village church, where they passed the night. About four o'clock the next morning a German officer told them they had better go to confession, as they would be shot half an hour later. About half-past four they were liberated. Shortly afterwards they were again arrested by a German brigade, which forced them to march before them in the direction of Malines. In reply to a question of one of the prisoners, a German officer said they were going to give them a taste of the Belgian quickfirers before Antwerp. They were at last released on the Thursday afternoon at the gates of Malines.

"It appears from other witnesses that several thousand male inhabitants of Louvain, who had escaped the shooting and the fire, were sent to Germany for a purpose which is still unknown to us.

"The fire at Louvain burned for several days. An eye-witness who left Louvain on 30th August gave the following description of the town at that time:

" 'Leaving Weert St. Georges,' he says, 'I only saw burned-clown villages and half-crazy peasants, who, on meeting anyone, held up their hands as a sign of submission. Before every house, even those burned down, hung a white flag, and the burned rags of them could be seen among the ruins.

" 'At Weert St. Georges I questioned the inhabitants on the causes of the German reprisals, and they affirmed most positively that no inhabitant had fired a shot, that in any case the arms had been previously collected, but that the Germans had taken vengeance on the population because a Belgian soldier belonging to the Gendarmerie had killed a Uhlan.

" 'The population still remaining in Louvain in the suburb of Heverie, where they were extremely crowded. They have been cleared out of the town by the troops and the fire.

"The fire started a little beyond the American College, and the town is entirely destroyed, except for the Town Hall and the station. Furthermore, the fire was still burning today, and the Germans, far from taking any steps to stop it, seemed to feed it with straw, an instance of which I observed in the street adjoining the Town Hall. The Cathedral and the theatre are destroyed and have fallen in, as also the Library; in short, the town has the appearance of an ancient ruined city, in the midst of which only a few drunken soldiers move about, carrying bottles of wine and liqueurs, while the officers themselves, seated in armchairs round the tables, drink like their men.

" 'In the streets the swollen bodies of dead horses rot in the sun, and the smell of fire and putrefaction pervades the whole place.'

"The Commission has not yet been able to obtain information about the fate of the Mayor of Louvain and of the other notables who were taken as hostages."

So much for the Belgian official account.

Of the line which the German attempt to cover up this hideous crime will take we have an indication in a German official paper, *The Friend of the People*, published in French and German at Liége for the enlightenment of the Belgians. It printed in September last a German account of the entry into Louvain and the story of a great plot of the Louvain people to murder all the German soldiers that night.

The story is transparently a lie. Its details of the gay, cheerful appearance that Louvain presented on the day of entry as a mask for the murderous plan I can deny from my own observation, as I left Louvain that day in the rear of the Belgian Army with a pitiable crowd of refugees from Tirlemont, whose tales of ruthlessness there set everyone fleeing from Louvain who could possibly do so. Before a single German entered, Louvain was desolate and in mourning, and abandoned by a great part of its population.

But the German account speaks of crowded *cafés* and animated streets.

In recoding the massacre of the inhabitants as having happened that very night owing to a treacherous uprising of the inhabitants the Germans again lie clumsily, for there is the clearest proof that it happened seven days afterwards.

But perhaps the following can be accepted as a fairly truthful German account of their own doings in Louvain, which follows the untruthful apologetic. It reads: "Our force concentrates at the railway station and opens fire on the houses around them and on other houses. We fire on the windows, force open the doors. The inhabitants are killed or dragged out, and the houses are burned. In a little while Louvain is in flames. At first we thought that the greater part of its inhabitants had been killed in the flames, for all who showed themselves in the streets received bullets. But after our return we found ladders placed in such a fashion as to facilitate the escape from the houses by their gardens at the rear. A very great number thus were saved, another proof that this attack on us had been prepared beforehand. That night at Louvain was a very grave experience, and we were lucky to get out of it so well."

A resolute effort to manufacture evidence to hide the truth as to Louvain can be expected from the German Government, which is at last awake to the harm done to the cause of Germany by brutalities which have shocked the civilized world. An indication of how evidence can be manufactured was provided in Brussels during September. One Thursday morning at the *Place des Palais* a battalion of Prussian soldiers paraded before the Palais Royal, at the windows of which German men and women waved handkerchiefs joyously. Meanwhile a cinematograph film was taken. One could intelligently foresee the future German dissemination of moving pictures showing the Brussels population welcoming eagerly the arrival of the Prussian Army!

On this point of German evidence the German excuses of "military necessity" for the wilful destruction of Rheims Cathedral should be examined in the light of their Belgian actions.

It is not open to any question that at Louvain the Germans burned the church of St. Pierre deliberately, whilst sparing other buildings. There had been then no Belgian troops in Louvain for many days. At Aerschot the Germans, *after* military occupation, destroyed part of Notre Dame with gunpowder, attempted to burn it, and desecrated it. At Termonde the Germans burned down the church after military occupation. Finally at Malines, during the successive bombardments, the Cathedral was made the principal object of attack, and nine-tenths of the shells discharged at the city fell in the Cathedral or in its vicinity. During these bombardments no Belgian troops were in Malines.

I will not attempt to deal with other horrors of the German occupation of Belgium at the same length, but will confine myself to a brief note of some of the worst as to the truth of which I was able to satisfy myself.

A gentleman who was in Dinant during August gave me the following account, which agreed substantially with the evidence of two other eye-witnesses. On August 15th, when the first big combat took place around Dinant, the town suffered somewhat from shell-fire, but its great misfortunes only began when the French evacuated the district under orders for a general retirement. On the night of August 21st a German armoured motor-car came into Dinant by the Rue St. Jacques, and without any reason began firing promiscuously in the street and at the houses. Many citizens were killed by this fire. A girl was mortally wounded in her cot. An innkeeper and his wife who opened their door to see what was going on were both killed. A gas-worker going out to his work was killed on his threshold. The assassins followed up their fire by throwing incendiary bombs at the houses and then went away.

That was the prelude of greater horrors. Next day a German force entered the town. The doors of the houses were forced open, men were killed, and women were driven, with their hands up, into an abbey, where for three days they were imprisoned without food, except some carrots which they had. Some workers in a cloth factory, of which the director, M. Himmer, was murdered, took refuge in a drain. They were discovered and all shot as they cowered in their hiding-place. At the Brewery Nicaise, in the suburb of St. Pierre, the workers, with their employers, two venerable brothers both aged over seventy, hid in the cellars of a brewery, and being discovered, were all killed. At the Place d'Armes, in front of the prison, two hundred men were collected by the Germans, and to make the slaughter quicker they were mowed down by a machine-gun. The people thus murdered were aged from twelve years to seventy-five years.

These wholesale murders took place in the suburbs of Leffe, St. Pierre, and St. Nicholas chiefly. In the central quarter of the town the rage for slaughter was not so furious. Hostages were taken and driven out of the town almost naked to the Ardennes. Then the town was systematically burned. On August 23rd hardly a vestige of it remained. The German officer in charge of these operations was said to be named Oberleutnant Beeger.

The story of Aerschot is not so clear as the story of Louvain, but it is certain that, whatever was excusable of reprisal in that town on the part of the Germans, there was a gross addition of causeless cruelty. The Germans first entered Aerschot on August 19th. Early in the occupation a German officer was killed by the son of Burgomaster Tieleman. According to some statements the officer had violated, or attempted to violate, his sister. It is impossible to ascertain with certainty the truth on this point. But if it is allowed that the Germans were fully justified in executing the lad, his father and his uncle (as they did), can the act of that lad be held to excuse three weeks of a savage and beastly cruelty towards the whole town?

On September 10th, the Germans having been driven out of Aerschot for a time, I was able to witness the results of their sacrilege and cruelty. It had been three weeks exactly since the Germans occupied the town. During that time they destroyed the greater part of it, desecrated the Church of Notre Dame, and murdered and tortured a great number of the inhabitants. On the first day of entry they attacked the Church of Notre Dame, bursting in its door with explosives, and endeavouring to set fire to all the woodwork, smashing images, pictures and pews, and looting the vestry. No scruple of religion stood in the way of desecration, which in some respects is too abominable to detail. Having pillaged and partly destroyed the church, the Germans set it aside as a prison for the inhabitants. Men and women were herded into it each night, and released in the morning. After a week of fury and cruelty, the German rage took a new turn, and all the men of the village were shut up permanently in the church night and day. The beautiful church as I have seen it-partly burned, partly destroyed, its floors stained, its images bespattered with the blood of victims of the Germans, its altars befouled-is an unforgettable monument of the German spirit.

By the side of the sacrilege committed in the church, the human torture and slaughter in other places in the town seem less horrible.

But in all one hundred and sixty-one people were shot at Aerschot, including the Burgomaster, his son, and his brother. Every house was looted, and most of the houses were burned.

At Aerschot, as elsewhere, the Germans seemed to have shown a special hatred of the churches and of the clergy. I may not recount all the story of their cruelties. Much of it must be kept for closed doors and the ears of judges and avengers. But two incidents! In the church which they made a prison, the German soldiers allowed a woman to be delivered of a child without aid, without so much as a screen. The curé of Gelrode, whom they had taken prisoner, they bound to a wall and then forced his men parishioners, at the point of the bayonet, to file before him and insult him grossly-I cannot be more exact. Then the priest was shot. Trying to find if in any particular way he had offended the Huns, I could discover nothing. He was of the Red Cross, and doubtless, like many of his cloth, he had gone into the trenches to comfort and solace his flock, and had helped with the wounded.

But never have I seen a priest with a weapon, never (with experience of at least a score of combats) seen them act otherwise than in strict fidelity to their healing office. Patriots they are without an exception, and their sermons are weapons of might to encourage the Belgians. But they are Christian priests also, and in my observation have never lifted the material arm against the Germans.

Yet they are clearly objects of special hatred and vengeance. Their churches are defiled and destroyed. Many are murdered, tortured; all are insulted. Why? I can suggest no other reason than the instinctive consciousness on the part of the Germans, that in this war against all that is gracious in our civilization Christianity is an enemy to be attacked through its ministers and its temples. For what other reason the special persecution of the priests, for what other reason the special destruction and the swinish desecration of churches which in some cases have been sanctified with the prayers of centuries?

Coming back to Malines after visiting Aerschot on September 10th, a priest of whom I had asked these questions endeavoured to answer them. He was an old friend. I met him first at Malines one day when the first wave of refugees from sacked Louvain flowed through there. He had come with some of his flock, and had tried to sustain them in their flight. His cassock, I noted, was dripping with wet, as if he had been in a storm of rain, but it was from the sweat of agony that the horrors of a night and a day had drawn from him. That day he was wild and distraught, thinking that no more was left for men but to hope for the mercy of the next world. Today he was more calm, and confessed quite simply that that day he had thought Antichrist was come; but now he knew that the war was only a trial through which the world was passing and which would soon be finished.

In answer to my questions he said that the clergy had been from the beginning of the war very patriotic. How could it have been otherwise when their people were attacked?

But before the war they had been, on the whole, very anti-militarist, not believing it possible that Belgium-"an innocent lamb in the fields, my son"-could be attacked. When the war broke out, the young priests went to the front as Red Cross assistants, nurses, chaplains; the old priests stayed at the base hospitals, and also helped to collect funds for the poor. Certainly the priests went into the trenches, but it was to administer the Sacraments to the soldiers as they went into action. He could guess no reason why the Germans should hate the priests so particularly. "And the beautiful churches, they truly have done nothing wrong!" His eyes filled with tears as he recalled his Louvain church.

Ending the conversation, the priest came back to a note of hope and consolation. "It is what God has permitted in His inscrutable wisdom. In the end good will come of it. I see good now. The people in their distress are turning to God. 'It is one of those occasions when, if there had not been a God, we would have been obliged to invent one.'

Europe will be purged of much evil of disbelief and indifference after this fiery trial. There will be a great revival of religion. In the fullness of time it will be seen that all the wrong that man has done will be repaired, and only the good will remain." It is a comfort truly-such simple faith.

Termonde claims a special place in the record of German brutality in Belgium because of the evidence it affords of the systematic preparation by Germany for war on the lines of incendiarism, pillage and murder. After great difficulties, owing to the destroyed bridges and flooded areas, I reached Termonde the day after its destruction, and found it almost entirely in ruins. Of one thousand five hundred houses not one hundred survived. Hospitals, homes for the poor, churches-all had been burned out. In one case at least a sick old man was burned in his bed.

Previous experience of the campaign in Belgium (wherein the Germans had achieved the distinction of having killed more of the civil population than of soldiers) had inured me to scenes of devastation. The ruins of Termonde could not have excited much attention were it not for the proof provided by the abandoned matériel of the Germans, and the unanimous testimony of the inhabitants, that the Emperor's Army was, as part of its training for war, drilled in systematic incendiarism, and as part of its equipment carried to the front special machinery for burning down towns.

Termonde was destroyed for much the same reason as Louvain. On September 4th, a German force came back from the field after a severe beating by the Belgians, and the German Commander, Sommerfeld, announced: "It is our duty to burn the town." The inhabitants were given two hours to quit, and then with well-drilled precision, companies of German soldiers marched through the streets breaking windows on each side with rifles as they marched. They were followed by two files of men with machines, which sprayed kerosene through the broken windows. Most of these spraying machines were operated by hand, but one at least was a big engine of arson driven by motor power. The next step was for soldiers to pass along throwing lighted fuses on the kerosene. Termonde was thus systematically destroyed. Two of the abandoned spraying machines l saw. All the inhabitants of Termonde gave the same version of its destruction.

The sack of the town was not marked by massacre, but eighty civic notables were taken away as prisoners to Germany, and there were a few incidental murders, and the Abbé de Carte, Dean of Lokeren, stated that the German soldiers not only set fire to the houses, but pursued women and children, tore from them their jewels, and killed some.

When the German Army retired, the people of Termonde came back promptly to their ruined homes. Perhaps it will not be counted too trivial to record an incident showing the wonderful cheerfulness of the Belgian peasantry in their misfortunes. That afternoon near Termonde a Belgian woman reported to a officer that there were two Germans still in her cottage (which had escaped ruin). A squad of four soldiers under a corporal were at once despatched with her. They found two pigs which the Germans had overlooked in their pillage. The befooled soldiers had to smile and had not the heart to punish the woman for her joke.

One public treasure escaped the burning of Termonde-the stout little tower of the Hôtel de Ville with its renowned carillon of bells.

But German barbarism is thorough. After vacating the town the Germans directed their artillery on to the tower and brought its music-crowned head to the ground. This little freakish addition of hate hurt the people of the town more, I think, than the incendiary fury which had destroyed their homes. The music of the carillons is the national music of the Flemings and in happier days the bellmaster was one of the most important of every town's officials. It was his duty from his eyrie near the sky, on feast-days, holy-days and all occasions of rejoicing, to make music which was bounded by no mean confines of walls and roofs, but surged over street and field to the farthest limits of sound. That the Germans should shoot down the sweet bells of Termonde which had given joy and consolation for centuries, showed a fiendish and ignoble malice.

Towards the end of September, I assisted at a calculation made by careful examiners regarding the total murders of civilians in those parts of Belgium invaded by the Germans where investigation by the Belgians had been possible. (The figures regarding places occupied by the Germans but still closed to investigation were not included.) In the Province of Liége at least 500 were massacred, mostly in the towns of Visé, Hervé, and Huy. In the Province of Brabant at least 1,100 were killed, of whom 600 belonged to Louvain and the others to Aerschot, Tirlemont, Diest, and Haecht. In the Province of Namur 1,500 were massacred, the chief contributors being the towns of Dinant and Andenne. In the Limburg and Luxemburg Provinces the losses were not so great, being about 350 in all. In the Province of Hainaut over 1,200 were killed, and the total, with other places, was at least 5,000. That was the record of actual direct murders. The indirect killing of the civilian population by the destruction of their homes and their food supplies was enormously greater.

The German army on the final reckoning before Heaven will have to account for the miserable deaths of at least 100,000 civilians-men, women and children, sacrificed not to military necessity but to wantonness of cruelty.

CHAPTER VII

STILL UNDISMAYED

THE uneasiness felt in Antwerp on account of the Zeppelin raids and the German campaign of atrocity at Louvain and elsewhere was not allowed to dismay the military command. All through September there was a cheerful and plucky effort to withstand the invader and to push him back from any district where his grip showed a sign of relaxing. The "secret history" of September cannot yet be told fully.

When it is told it will provide another great proof of the moral courage of Belgium. Threatened by land and air, subjected to all the ruthless pressure of war, and furthermore made the victims of a policy of massacre, the Belgians refused steadily to give the promise that was asked of them to allow immunity to the German lines of communication. Perhaps the history of the operations in the North of France would have been different if at this critical point the Germans had been able to conquer the heroic resolution of the Belgians: for Belgium immobilized a vast army which otherwise would have been employed on the movement towards Paris.

What was particularly lovable – I find that the right wordabout the Belgian courage in days was its cheerfulness and its eagerness to rejoice with a friend. I remember when the news of the British naval victory in the Heligoland reached Antwerp there was great rejoicing. The General Staff promptly communicated it to every military post in the province. It was very touching to see how, in the midst of their own miseries, the Belgian people entered so whole-heartedly into congratulations to their ally.

There sprang up a feeling almost of cheerfulness in Antwerp. People embraced in the streets, exclaiming: "Ah, soon the English will have the German ships all in the cellar of the codfish" (the local Davy Jones's locker). They magnified the event far more than their own recent victory at Malines. The absence of all jealously and frank gratitude for help are admirable traits of the Belgian people. Clearly they will emerge from the war strengthened greatly in character.

To give another instance of the same spirit. Late in September a party of British naval aviators reached Antwerp with the plan to attack the German Zeppelin sheds at Düsseldorf and Cologne. The Belgians at once set themselves with eagerness to co-operate in the adventure. The distance from Antwerp to Düsseldorf was rather great for a single flight; so the Belgians formed an advance base for the aviators at Bourg Leopold, sending out quite a herd of armoured motor-cars and a company of carabineer cyclists.

Leaving at dawn, the corps of aviators flew without mis-adventure to this base. The weather was clear and there was a little wind. At the base they divided into two parties, one party going to attack the Zeppelin hangars at Düsseldorf, the other to attack the hangars at Cologne. As far as the River Meuse the weather continued clear and favourable, but after the Meuse fog was encountered. The aviator having Cologne as his objective became enveloped in a thick fog. For an hour and a half he circled around and finally, by an accident, dropped a bomb on the Dutch town of Maestricht. (The British Government afterwards apologized for this.)

The second aviator, having Düsseldorf as his objective, was more fortunate. The town was found enveloped in mist, but not fog. Descending very low, the aviator was able to distinguish the Zeppelin hangar, and discharged all his bombs upon it. That some effect was obtained he was sure, but he could not be certain that the flames which broke out were quelled or not. He was afraid that, owing to the low elevation at which he discharged his bombs (about four hundred feet) some of them did not explode owing to the operation of the time safety fuse, which is intended to safeguard against explosions so premature as to damage the aeroplane discharging the bombs. But partial success was achieved.

Both aviators returned to the base or near to it, finding armoured motor-cars waiting to convoy them. All reached Antwerp safely the same night, and that night they were out scouting for a Zeppelin which had been reported over Antwerp; but found nothing but a comet. The commander of the aviators,

Major Gerard, spoke to me with enthusiasm of the skilful and eager manner in which the Belgians had helped him.

To return to a record of the events of September in their chronological order: early in the month there came-inspired by terror because of the sack of Louvain – crowds of refugees into the Antwerp fortified area. A constant stream flowed towards the city of pitiful victims of the fright engendered by German barbarity. But it was of paramount necessity that the fortress authorities should refuse further additions to the population, which already exceeded the possibilities of house accommodation, and it was necessary to divert the stream towards the coast.

I recorded in my diary on September 1st:

"Fortunately the weather is fine and warm; if rain should come, the plight of the fugitives would be more terrible. Some arrive after marching forty miles, almost dead from hunger and fatigue. One thing this agony of Belgium is doing: it gives the spectator fortitude to endure. There is a sublime heroism in the Belgian people. They accept their martyrdom in the spirit of the early Christians, refusing to make a single concession in their patriotic faith, but neither making reprisals nor yielding to unmanly repinings.

"An impudent proposal has been made by the Germans to the effect that to save Malines the fort of Waelhem should be given up. The proposal was at once rejected. From all appearances it was not only a monstrous but also a 'bluffing' attempt at blackmail, for today the Germans seem to be falling back in the province of Antwerp, and there is absolutely reliable information that during Friday and Saturday trains sufficient to carry an army corps hurried east with German soldiers, going presumably from the Belgian theatre of operations towards Eastern Prussia.

"In the province of Antwerp, down to a line ten miles north of Brussels, the country is free of the German forces. Malines is no longer bombarded, and has suffered little. Heyst-op-den-Berg has been evacuated. Though an undefended town, it suffered a bombardment which partly destroyed the church and set fire to several buildings. From all the indications which I have (through official reports and through a tour of investigation I made yesterday) it seems likely that the outbreak of barbarism which made the week so terrible was due to a policy of desperation on the part of the Germans. If one could judge the course of the war from this centre it would be with the confidence that soon the tide of battle will turn."

With the aim, chiefly, of effecting a diversion in favour of the Allies, on September 5th the Belgian Staff decided that the time was ripe for a move forward and set on foot operations which brought the Belgians to the very environs of Louvain and inflicted a grave embarrassment on the German forces. The plan of the campaign was that from Antwerp as a centre two armies should move out south-west and south-east, and act as two blades of a shears; whilst the left blade-that to the south-east-kept its position, the other blade should close down upon it and on what German force remained between. The plan left to the generals in the field, as operations developed, the choice of an ultimate objective: Brussels, Louvain, or a point east of Louvain on the German line of communication to Liége.

The early operations were crowned with complete success, and by September 9th the Belgian Army was on a line from Malines to Aerschot, the enemy holding a triangle based on Brussels, Louvain, with its apex at Malines.

To hammer on the line Malines-Louvain was, then, the clear policy of the Belgian Army, and it was carried through to the accomplishment of what may be called an alternative success, the drawing away from other fields of great German forces.

On September 10th I went out to Aerschot and moved forward when a decisive phase of the action seemed to be developing. A Belgian gentleman, who is managing director of a big London business and who abandoned it to take his place in the ranks of soldiers, and whose post-of low rank but of great dignity-was that of cyclist-orderly to the major of a field battery, took me under his wing to the battery position at Wezemael. There were two cyclist-orderlies attached to this battery as messengers, and the other had just been killed by a shell, so on the law of averages it was a safe battery for a while. Desultory fighting had gone on all the morning, with the Belgians always attacking and the Germans keeping strictly to their trenches.

With the afternoon very strong German reinforcements, especially in howitzer artillery, came up, and just when the line of our infantry had made a good rush forward, high-explosive shell falling over the trenches in the main position intimidated some of the men, and there was a "break" for a while. The position was exciting. Possibly the "break" meant a general falling back, even a rout. The shell-fire was heavy enough to be disconcerting, but it did not seem fair to run back, as that would add to the difficulties of the officers with the soldiers. I sauntered-with as speedy a saunter as was consistent with an affectation of indifference – and had the reward of a grateful shout from one officer.

The "break" was fairly serious for a while and three guns were lost at that point. But the loss was soon repaired, and the Belgians went back and recovered the guns. They are good stuff, very good stuff, the Belgian men, and have plenty both of courage and wits, but their army is really only two years old, and so not at its adult strength in some respects.

The evening of September 10th, as the armies were going to rest during the hours of darkness, I returned to Antwerp, and came out to the same position in the morning of the 11th. That day was spent in manoeuvring for positions with the aid of artillery action all along the line. At Wazemael, the Belgian front had pushed forward some three kilometres, and I was able to get with a battery to a windmill on a hill on the left-hand side of the road leading from Aerschot to Louvain. The day was wet and cold, and severely trying to the infantry in the trenches condemned to alert inaction. On this left flank even the artillery had little to do, as its duty was to hold its ground while the centre and the right wing swung around towards it.

Towards evening the sky cleared a little and the distant tower of Malines Cathedral showed in a haze of gold and red like an accusing arm raised to Heaven to call for vengeance on the German desecrators: and on the other flank of the German front the ruins of Louvain showed startlingly clear, the dainty little spires of the Hôtel de Ville standing out of a wilderness of black ruins.

It was, it seemed, the moment for an advance which would rush over all obstacles of time and space to exact quick punishment; and, truly enough, a general movement forward of our infantry seemed to be in progress. But no wild, daring night attack carried us in on its wave to Louvain that night. To have attempted it would probably have been unwise. This modern warfare is too coldly scientific a matter to allow of such exploits.

With nightfall the soldiers sought straw from the fields and made rough bivouacs. In a peasant's hut I rested until three in the morning, getting for supper a glass of milk won from a cow which had been hidden in a ditch and so escaped the Germans, and a slice of country bread, largely made of sand. With the first of the dawn of the 12th, the Belgians marched forward, and so little serious seemed to be the opposition of the Germans at this stage that – unwittingly getting ahead of the Belgian advance – I was within eight kilometres of Louvain (on foot) without being fired at, and got near to Mr. Mooring's château, of Vrouwenpark, which the Germans had "sacked" some time before with hoggish rage against its pictures, marbles and tapestries. A Belgian motor-cyclist came to bring me back, and I went to the windmill on the hill again and then at six a.m. saw the battle line unfold along Haecht, Werchter, Bostecher. Again the work was mostly with artillery, and as the day developed there did not seem a chance to push home a vital attack.

As the Belgian advance developed in seriousness it was plain that the German commander was obtaining strong reinforcements, and at one point he seemed about to develop a counterattack by attempting to envelop the Belgian left wing. The attempt was not persevered in, and the general character of the day's fighting along the whole line was a persistent Belgian attack, answered by a stubborn German resistance, which sometimes held its ground and sometimes had to yield. The conclusion to me seemed obvious, that the Germans had now brought up their strength to the utmost point that was judicious in view of the general situation of the campaign, and that it was more than doubtful whether they would be able to hold their own in the new attacks which the Belgians, with replenished troops and renewed confidence, were launching. The general impression given during this first great attacking movement on the part of the Belgian Army was that the strategic disposition was excellent. Certainly it took the Germans by surprise on the first two days, and the co-ordination of the various divisions was happily timed.

Late in the afternoon I quitted the left flank position and motored forty kilometres to get to the right flank, where King Albert was at the head of the troops pushing out from Malines. It was possible here to observe the good work done by the new howitzers with which the Belgian artillery had been reinforced. A Belgian field battery, too, was doing finely, and the German batteries in reply were firing at a point one thousand yards to the right of it, until, unfortunately, the "slackness" of some Red Cross officers allowed a little group of people-who had no legitimate business there-to show themselves openly against the sky-line on an embankment in front of the left flank of the battery. The enemy naturally guessed something, and a few minutes afterwards that battery was smothered in shell and had to move. (Belgian officers in high command afterwards exacted much more stringent precautions against Red Cross assistants, and the like, thus endangering military positions.)

Here and there a shortage of infantry officers was being felt. The personal influence of King Albert, who was constantly at the front, was very marked. One incident of this day might well have been unfortunate, when a hard-pressed infantry brigade began to give ground. It so happened that King Albert was at that point, and supplied just the extra moral force necessary to push the tide of victory forward.

Leaving the battlefield on Saturday evening (September 12th), the position looked good for a final advance on Sunday, though I had a subconscious feeling that the evening of Friday had been the moment for a crowning victory: for obviously during the Saturday the Germans had got further reinforcements. Sunday brought its disappointment. After a wild night of storm and rain the Germans, with the dawn-possibly with fresh troops brought up from Liége-developed an attempt to cut the line between Antwerp and Aerschot, coming from the direction of Heyst-op-den-Berg. The Belgian command decided to be satisfied with the *terrain* and the prestige already won, and went back to the defensive.

The final impression left on me by this phase of the campaign was that with just one more ounce of driving force, this Belgian Army, with its cheerful courage, its admirable equipment, its good strategic leadership, would have had the Germans out of Louvain and Brussels. If there could have been put a few thousand British Tommies side by side with them to give them just another ounce of drive!

The Belgian soldier at Antwerp, who had been promised French support or British support, during many days of weary fighting against great odds was always asking pathetically, "When are the British coming?" He felt lonely and in the dark faced by this huge German Army. If I had been Belgian commander-in-chief I would have dressed up a regiment of recruits in British uniforms and marched them round just to give the Belgians the illusion that they were not alone.

My diary on Sunday, September 14th, recorded (the effort to be as optimistic as possible will be noted):

"The Belgian Army rests for a time. There is naturally some local disappointment that a week of great effort was not crowned with the capture of Louvain. But the soldiers can be satisfied that the main objective of the movement was achieved. That objective was to harass, alarm and weaken the enemy, and on the Russian front as well as the Franco-British front the benefit of the Belgian advance was felt.

" The effect of the movement on Louvain by the Belgian Army was to offer to the Germans two alternatives, either to withdraw great bodies of troops from other points for its defence or to allow our army to establish itself on its line of retreat. In choosing the first alternative the German commanders seem to give an indication of their state of mind. If they did not contemplate the possibility of an early retreat, it is likely they would have refused to withdraw an army from other points to meet the Belgians, trusting to retrieve the position at Louvain later. As it was, the Germans seem to have collected no less than two Army Corps around Louvain. These, holding a strongly entrenched position, were able to make it clear to the Belgian commanders that to pursue the attack was injudicious. On Sunday, with their new troops, the Germans developed a very threatening movement to envelop the extreme Belgian left. Our troops at once took up a new line to meet this development, but on Sunday evening it was decided to rest content for the present.

"Today the hammering of the Germans by our troops ceased, and both sides took a rest. Traversing the Belgian line during the morning and afternoon, I found the men happy and confident. When the next call comes they will be ready. It is significant that the Germans seem to have welcomed the truce eagerly and made no counter-attack today."

That was "putting the best face on it" (though all the facts were true). But I own now that I went back to Antwerp that Sunday night grievously sick with mere chagrin. The requital of the horrors of Louvain – horrors which still, after many nights, haunted my sleep-had seemed so near. I had bivouacked on the battlefield within two hours' walk of the ravished city, keeping the wakeful hours happy with the thought of how civilization would be vindicated and barbarism rebuked by the Belgian entry into the city. Now we were back to the defence of Antwerp's fortified position.

I spent most of the week of sickness that followed writing letters to people in London, urging that 20,000 British troops should be spared somehow to come to the help of the Belgians. The Belgian Army at this stage numbered about 120,000. With the addition of 20,000 British infantry it would have made a perfect army of 140,000, all emulous in courage and hardihood. The Belgians wanted, oh, so pathetically they wanted! – to see a friendly uniform. And British troops sent among these scenes of horror and outrage on women and children would have fought, as our men fought in the Indian Mutiny, to win against any odds. We would take back Louvain, Brussels, establish ourselves on the Germans' lines of communication, do more good by sending 20,000 to the rear of the German than 40,000 to the front of him.

All this I wrote, and more. Wildness perhaps? It was difficult to be sober and soundly cautious under the circumstances. At any rate I was snubbed by the strategists and the conclusion was come to that Antwerp must dree its own weird. I felt a strong foreboding. The Germans, almost beaten by this attack, would surely now in prudence see that the Belgian threat was once for all removed from their flank.

How near the attack of September was to success this entry from my diary will show:

"Near Louvain, September 11th.

"The victorious advance of the Belgian Army continues. I write this late in the afternoon at a windmill on the extreme left of the Belgian position, from which one may see what buildings have been left standing in Louvain.

"From this windmill for a distance of about thirty kilometres stretches the line of the Belgian advance.
The men are confident and eager, and the light of battle is in the fiery eyes of the little Ardennes horses which serve so gallantly in the cavalry and artillery.

"It seems likely that this evening or tomorrow Louvain will be again in Belgian hands, and the Germans will pay another item in the long account with these people.

"But there are indications that stubborn fighting will decide the issue. The Germans, though they were heavily reinforced yesterday, and probably are getting fresh troops up now, are sitting down strictly on the defensive.

"At 4 p.m., with eager Belgian troops facing them and artillery searching their positions, they make no reply, but hold themselves within entrenchments.

"In the country saved during the past two days from the Germans, the work of reparation goes on confidently. Aerschot church has been almost cleared of *débris* and filth. In some of the streets which were not destroyed the townspeople have returned and busy themselves cleaning the streets and collecting remnants of furniture."

I was never "near Louvain" again. The German power asserted itself and the fall of Antwerp was soon to follow. But the optimism of that week was justifiable. During the first fortnight in September the Germans had allowed their strength in Northern Belgium to decline dangerously. Some papers I found on German prisoners at Aerschot gave valuable indications of this. An order of the day of September 3rd by the German commander at Aerschot stated: "It has come to my knowledge that many men think that the use of the Landsturm in the country of the enemy is not provided for by the German laws. That interpretation is false. Without doubt, according to the law, the Landsturm should first be utilized in the home garrison, but after the Imperial proclamation which has appeared, the Landsturm can be employed in the enemy's country. Our men ought to be warned that in this war the actual existence of Germany is at stake. Consequently it is indispensable that all members of the Landsturm should be called to service during the war. During these last days some men have shown signs of cowardice. The penalty for that is death."

The position north of Brussels was held largely by these disaffected Landsturm soldiers up to September 10th.

Some very interesting details concerning the Belgian advance, as it was seen from the German side, were communicated to me later by a Belgian who was in Brussels all that week.

The German force holding Brussels and Louvain, about 60,000 strong, were, he said, very effectively entrenched behind the segment of a circle beginning south-east of Termonde and ending close to Wavre. The trenches were very deep-roofed, with galleries, and reinforced with iron rails and cement.

Such grave fear was entertained by the German commanders during the Belgian attack that the German General Staff for the Brussels district was removed from the city and stationed somewhere south. At one point the Belgian advance got within eight miles of Brussels, and the Belgian shells fell around the German observation balloon. The inhabitants of Brussels went out to the northern heights and watched the advance, and, when no German observers were present, cheered at the burst of each Belgian shell. A temporary cessation of the Belgian operations came as a great relief to the Germans, whose position, in spite of the reinforcements they had wrung out of their headquarters staff, was fast becoming desperate.

After September 14th the German Army around Brussels was reinforced again and moved up its line from Wavre, and was shaping as if for an advance between Alost and Termonde, or for the strengthening of its defensive line there. Two very heavy pieces of cannon, I heard, passed through Brussels from the south and were sent north towards Malines.

Meanwhile the Belgian Army did not give up hope. Quite the contrary. On September 17th I was able to record:

"Advantage has been taken of the few days' rest to effect some changes in the Belgian Army, which will undoubtedly bring about a strengthening and stiffening for the next campaign, which may be looked for very soon.

"Previously I have commented on the shortage of infantry officers. This was due in part to the state of things existing at the outbreak of the war, so treacherously and unexpectedly forced upon Belgium, but in the greater part to the undue wastage of officers owing to their conspicuous uniforms and courage. After Tirlemont many infantry regiments were almost without company officers. The losses were made good from reserves and by the promotion of non-commissioned officers, but still the position was that the best could not be got out of the splendid material because the ranks of the officers were so weak.

"Now a bold and original method has been adopted to remedy the deficiency. The élite of the officers of the gendarmerie have been drafted into the infantry as company officers. They are men of high character, accustomed to lead, with experience in handling men, and will without doubt make excellent infantry officers. There have been some other changes which I need not detail, and the artillery has been largely reinforced with heavy howitzers."

Indeed, the impression of optimism given by the failure of the Germans to follow up the retirement of the Belgians behind the Antwerp forts was so strong that I found myself a week later investigating the living conditions of the poor in Antwerp and recording (September 20th):

"Now the winds from the east whisper of the winter coming. In the parks the leaves decay and fall. The sunshine has lost all its languor and shows a hard brightness; when the sky is overcast or weeping, the air is actually cold. Less than a month ago we were complaining in Antwerp of the hardship of staying under roofs during sweltering August nights, and counting it as one of the minor misfortunes of war that apparently the big gun-fire had frightened away the swallows and, consequently, the mosquitoes were more than ordinarily troublesome. Like little Zeppelins hovering in the air, vicious, alert, they made it a misery to gather by the river bank, as the poor of Antwerp loved to do, seeking messages of hope in the flowing water.

"No more mosquitoes, no more Zeppelins (apparently) now, since the equinoctial gales blew away to the south the last of the heat, and we come face to face with the winter. How will it fare with the poor in this city, where the Belgian nation takes refuge until the storm is over and the Huns have been driven away? It is good to be able to say the cheerful thing. Many woes the Belgians have suffered because they were faithful to their trust; but among them will not be the woe of famine over territory where the Belgian flag still flies. Of the districts where the Germans are in possession one can say nothing. They have suffered: they will continue to suffer until the day of deliverance. But here the Belgians know that their King is a true shepherd of his people; that the Government will allow none to starve; that in the face of ravaging war the nation has become a family; and that, last, though not least, civilized Europe has had enough gratitude to help with loans and gifts the gallant sentinel nation which withstood the first and most savage blow of the war.

"During a day's tour of the poor quarters of the town, where hive the dock workers and the like, I found no distress at all. Many have to eat the bread of charity for the present. But bread they have.

A. is a docker with wife and three children, one of them an infant. He has had no work since the war broke out. Before, he earned nine francs or ten francs a day. Now the family get three francs fifty centimes a week in cash from a relief committee; the boys sell papers and earn between them about eight francs a week. For the women and children there is provided a free meal at mid-day. So they manage.

"B. is the young wife with two children of a soldier at the war. He gets one and a half francs a day. She goes out 'charing,' and earns two francs a day. She puts the children in a home during the day, where they get a mid-day meal of soup eked out with bread and butter, which they bring themselves. This crèche is conducted on kindergarten lines, and the little ones learn to make baskets.

"C. is the wife of a carter who gets a little work for the army now, but his regular work was stopped by the war. She works outside her home three days a week to help the family budget. They had a little money saved up and that is now a standby. At the opening of the war there was a food panic, and they rushed to a shop and bought one hundred pounds of rice and fifty pounds of white beans.

Now they eat these very, very sadly, because all sorts of food are cheaper than before. Having bought the rice and the beans, however, they must eat them for thrift's sake.

"One more typical family. D. is a widow with a grown-up daughter and a little boy. The mother keeps a small shop. The daughter is a 'coster' selling vegetables from a barrow in the mornings, stewed apples and pears in the afternoons, mussels on Wednesdays and Fridays. This widow reckoned herself rich enough to help the soldiers a little.

"These are examples. All I saw was encouraging, suggesting good thrift and providence on the part of the poorer classes, excellent management on the part of the Government and Municipality to give the best help at the least cost, cheerful patience and charity on the part of the people. The British and the Americans have done something to help the poor of Belgium from suffering further privations and miseries. It should please them to know that their help is appreciated, and that it is used with careful management to the very best advantage."

But all this cheerfulness was vanity. Antwerp was doomed. Behind a mask of sloth the Germans were bringing up their fatal great artillery.

CHAPTER VIII

ANTWERP ATTACKED

THE siege of Antwerp might be said to have begun the day that Brussels fell. But leaving out of consideration now the more or less desultory operations of late August and early September, the Germans began a serious attack on the second capital of Belgium on Sunday, September 27th. After the failure of the Belgian attempt to recover Louvain (September 5th to September 13th) the Germans, convinced that the Belgian Army could not be threatened into staying at home, decided to turn it out of its last stronghold.

On September 26th news came of a German movement in advance from the direction of Alost. This movement was promptly met by our troops, who, pushing onward from the north-west, swept the country clean of the Germans right up to Alost. There was some very interesting skirmishing during the day in connection with this sweeping movement, not of great military importance as far as the numbers engaged were concerned, but useful in showing the unrelaxed courage of the Belgian troops.

The first skirmish of the day I did not see, but the second, at the village of Erpe, was lively enough to be worthy of record. A German outpost had established itself in a little copse after the Germans had been driven out of Erpe, and our carabineer cyclists and Lancers were engaged for a couple of hours in digging them out. Ultimately a field battery was drawn into the fight, and the copse was soon cleared, several German prisoners being taken and a few Germans killed. Another outpost near Alost was engaged by carabineer cyclists with the help of an armoured motor-car and satisfactorily crushed. An interesting indication of the eagerness of all ranks was the presence of the general of division (General De Wit) in the very front of the line with an armoured motor-car. When the rifle-fire from the German outpost began suddenly, he gave the order to the men *"Ne bougez pas,"* and saw them disposed effectively to deal with the enemy, while he himself stayed to fight the little action through.

That evening marked the close of the fortnight since the operations which brought the Belgian Army so close to Louvain. It had been a fortnight of outpost fighting and daring reconnaissance on the part of the Belgian Army, with the infantry very little engaged, but with the cavalry, cyclists, and artillery almost constantly at work. After the cessation of our strong offensive a fortnight before some return of the offensive had been expected from the Germans. That expectation apparently had not been realized. They had taken up, seemingly, the attitude of a besieged force, and when they had made sorties had promptly withdrawn on meeting a vigorous opposition. With the single exception of Aerschot all the towns taken from the Germans from September 5th to September 13th had been held, and in addition some new territory had been cleared. The total area of Belgium freed from the Germans had indeed largely increased during the fortnight. Hardly a day had passed without some addition to the freed territory and some addition to the confidence and eagerness of the Belgians.

But all this was vain seeming. The Germans, behind a mask of timidity and withdrawal, were preparing for an irresistible attack on Antwerp. Whilst they were displaying weakness on each flank, in their centre they were preparing the movement which was to smash open a road to the citadel. But of this we in Antwerp had no suspicion, though our Intelligence Department had brought in news of the passage of great 28-centimetre howitzers through Brussels.

On September 29th, I put on record this as the prevailing impression in Antwerp:

"If one could overhear a discussion of the German General Staff regarding the position at Antwerp it would probably run somewhat on these lines:

"'We must manage somehow or other to get rid of the threats of that accursed Belgian Army. If we have to retreat to the Rhine it will be on our flank, and may cause us enormous losses. But how can we get rid of it? To take troops from the Aisne is impossible. To take them from

East Prussia is just as impossible. We have no men left to draw upon in Germany. Already we have to face grave grumblings for drawing upon the Landwehr for foreign service, and when we have drawn on the Landwehr they are not much use. Well, we had better try "bluff" again. We can spare a few big guns at least, and bombard Belgian towns from a distance. It will do some damage. And we will let the Belgian people know that we will cease fire if they will give us a pledge to stay at home with their army. They can keep their Antwerp if they will leave our lines alone. Perhaps the "bluff" will succeed. The Belgians must be sick by now of seeing their towns destroyed and their civilians massacred."'

In such spirit of confidence we awaited an attack which showed itself to be surely fatal as soon as it developed!

On September 26th the movement in advance on our right wing had carried us to the gates of Alost. The next afternoon Alost was taken by the Belgians, who by nightfall were carrying on a spirited cavalry advance in the direction of Brussels. Saturday's fighting (September 26th) I have already recorded. Late that evening the Belgian Lancers penetrated into Alost and were welcomed with joy by the inhabitants. Seizing the three bridges which cross the River Dendre at Alost and separate the small eastern portion of the town from the main quarter, the Belgian force rested content for the day.

During the night the Germans brought up reinforcements, and from the eastern or Brussels side of the river began an artillery and infantry attack. It was our day's task (September 27th) to dislodge them, and the task was carried through with spirited *élan* and tactical skill, which led to a success with little loss on our side, and heavy losses of killed and prisoners among the Germans.

This battle of Alost gave the best opportunity I have enjoyed as a war correspondent to see a modern action. It was "set" well from the point of view of the spectator. The Belgians, having by the surprise attack of Saturday night captured more than half the town and the bridges over the Dendre, the battle of Sunday developed along the river line, the Germans holding the houses on one side, the Belgians the houses on the other. The streets on our side were barricaded with barrels of salted herrings and with carts.

Our artillery was disposed along a ridge at the outskirts of the town, and-ignoring the enemy's batteries - bombarded fiercely the houses occupied by the Germans. The enemy's artillery followed their example and devoted all their fire to our infantry along the river line.

A friendly civic dignitary opened for me the tower staircase of the beautiful Town Hall of Alost, and from the top gallery, not one hundred yards from the river, I could watch every detail of the combat, even to the outflanking movement of our Lancers on the right wing. The Belgian artillery work was of the best. House after house occupied by the Germans was set on fire or torn open-blood-red clouds of dust coming from the roofing tiles as the shells exploded beneath. The German line was soon all ruins and flames. On the other hand, the German artillery was much at fault. It destroyed houses in which there were no soldiers, and my tower of observation-an obvious place for a hostile gunner to explore-was never touched. But when at lunch time I went back to the rear about two miles for a safe and comfortable eating-place, a German shell came within twenty yards of the wine-bottle.

At 1.30 the eastern side of the river was abandoned by the Germans, and the Belgians advanced. Up to nightfall a spirited but careful advance continued; but, alas, it was not the German Army that we were meeting at Alost, but some Landwehr units, whose only task was to engage attention whilst the real attack developed in the centre.

Several Belgian civilians were brought in after the action, wounded by our own fire, the Germans having put them in the front of their line. The streets, too, on the eastern side of the town, when the action was finished, were strewn with the corpses of civilians, almost equal in numbers to the corpses of the German soldiers. There is no doubt at all that they used civilians as barriers against the fire of the Belgians.

At the very time that the battle of Alost was being fought so cheerfully on our side, the first indication of the real German attack was given by a bombardment of Malines with 28-centimetre guns, which had been brought into position to attack the forts of Liezel, Waelhem and Wavre-St. Catherine. Malines had just been re-occupied by its civil population: Cardinal Mercier had returned to his ravaged church and palace; and his people were assembled in the cathedral at Mass to give thanksgiving that the city had been freed from the German invader, when the shells began to fall into the city. They were 28-centimetre, high-explosive shells, and inflicted enormous damage where they struck. A large house in the Grand Place near the cathedral collapsed into a heap of ruins when struck. Another shell falling in the street, tore a great pit in the earth and eviscerated a bystander, flinging his body fifty yards away.

The civil population, who had fled from Malines during its previous bombardment with much lighter artillery, and had returned when it seemed that the tide of German invasion was beginning to ebb, took again to wild flight as if pursued by the wrath of Heaven. These new great shells seemed like devastating thunderbolts and made all previous gun-fire appear trivial.

The bombardment was marked by the plucky behaviour of the 3rd Lancers, who were quartered in the old barracks near Malines Cathedral. Men saddled up in perfect coolness, and with the colonel at their head, marched out of the town at a walk. The pace was for the sake of the morale of the men, and for the sake of the fugitive civil population. This retirement under such great shell-fire was worthy of the best traditions of any army in the world.

Why the Germans bombarded Malines, an open city, on this Sunday morning, was not clear at first. It seemed just another instance of German policy, wreaking vengeance for military defeats by killing the civil population, and destroying private property. But as the siege of Antwerp developed, it became clear that the bombardment was part of a policy. All the thickly-populated centres around the citadel of Antwerp were bombarded in turn with the 28-centimetre shells, until the civil population was driven in upon the centre of the fortified area to embarrass its defence. Thus on October 1st Boom came under shell-fire from the Germans. From early dawn it had been filled with crowds of refugees from the villages in the south and west. At ten shells began to fall in the town among them, and set them in flight again, communicating a panic to the population of the town, who began to run out in all directions, sometimes without troubling to take any of their property. Boom is an industrial town almost purely devoted to the manufacture of bricks and tiles. The population was lacking in the stoical qualities of the agricultural villages. It showed a greater emotion of fear than I had before seen in Belgium. The screaming of the shells overhead was answered by the screams of women and frightened children. Very quickly the town poured out its population on the road leading to Antwerp. That seemed to be the result sought at by the Germans, for the bombardment then ceased. Some scores of civilians had been killed; but that was not the object aimed at. Many thousands of panic-stricken fugitives had been driven into Antwerp, already seriously overcrowded. That was the purpose to be achieved.

Throughout the week the same policy was pursued. Each day some open town was smashed up in part by the monstrous shells of the siege guns, and its terrified population sent crowding into Antwerp. On October 2nd, when I had a foreboding of the fall of the city, I recorded in my diary:

"If the final event proves that Antwerp city has decided not to endure the horrors of a bombardment, preferring the horrors of a German occupation, let no one dare a word of censure. These streams of fugitives choking the roads day after day, the aged trembling for their few remaining days, the nuns and monks breaking from their cloisters, the sick and the palsied carried by their friends, the women just risen from child-bed carrying their babes, the sobbing children-these streams are enough to drown the most heroic resolution. The Hun policy of the German Emperor, announced in the first instance for China, has been imposed with all its savagery on Belgium, and now is seen in its full horror by Antwerp.

Apart from the mental effect of seeing these uprooted families pouring into the inner fortress, the administration of the city is gravely preoccupied with the task of finding for them food and shelter. That humane work takes attention from other matters."

In recording the bombardment of Boom I have anticipated the calendar somewhat. The events of Sunday at Malines and elsewhere had filled Antwerp with a vague alarm rather than with a reasoned dread. In the field our operations that day had been singularly successful. On both flanks we had had some advance. From nowhere was any serious German infantry development reported. But those monstrous shells falling in Malines? Would they be able to reach farther afield? The crowds of refugees spread the dismay of this question to Antwerp.

Monday, September 28th, passed in quick fluctuations from dread to confidence. The German forces, under cover of their heavy artillery, made a slight general advance, taking Alost on one flank, Heyst-op-den-Berg on the other, and pushing their line up to Malines. An artillery attack was commenced by them upon the forts of the southern sector of the outer circle, that is to say, Liezel, Waelhem, Catherine-St. Wavre, and Lierre. The guns of the forts were reinforced by our field artillery and a heavy battery of British naval guns mounted on an armoured train. Thus the German attack, already directed at the strongest sector of the fortified area, was met by extra gun power, and this was probably known to the Germans, but they could not change the direction of their attack, because the heavy guns on which they chiefly relied had been put in position for this sector, and could not easily be moved.

Monday's operations showed no particular development. On Tuesday Fort Catherine-St. Wavre was put out of action. It is said that a shell found the magazine and thus destroyed the fort. Another account states that a German spy exploded the magazine. It is quite probable, but it is not necessary as an explanation. Clearly "modern" forts-cupolas and all-are not able to withstand the fire of the guns of 28-centimetres. The same day Fort Waelhem was damaged severely. The German artillery attack was succeeding with disconcerting quickness against the forts. It was, however, making little or no impression on the field artillery, neither the heavy pieces nor the light pieces, bearing out the argument that the best reply to heavy pieces in the field is the fire of other heavy pieces behind good earthworks.

On Wednesday, September 30th, the Germans, finding Catherine-St. Wavre Fort silent, concentrated their fire on

Waelhem Fort, with some incidental bombardment of the open town of Lierre. Waelhem Fort, gallantly commanded by Commandant De Wit, achieved a minor success during the day by a ruse. Pretending to be silenced, it brought some force of the enemy out into the open and there heavily punished them with its own fire and the fire of supporting batteries. But the effect of the monstrous German shells was being felt. Whatever the shells struck they destroyed. The elaborate machinery of the cupola forts, not designed to withstand such tremendous shocks, began to break down. The Belgian field artillery, like little Destroyers entering into an action of Dreadnoughts, gathered around the threatened fort and fired thickly their shells, preventing the enemy from bringing up any light field artillery.

On Wednesday afternoon at four o'clock the second disaster of the siege came. The German shells found the city waterworks, behind Waelhem Fort, and soon destroyed them, doubtless with full knowledge of what they were doing. Thereafter the city of Antwerp was without water. There was supposed to be an alternative supply to be drawn from the Scheldt Canals. It never appeared up to the end of the siege in sufficient quantity to keep the underground drainage in circulation, though after some days a little brackish water could be drawn from the mains.

A field battery (the 8th) was almost drowned out by the rush of water from the destroyed reservoir. It was extricated under shell-fire with adroitness and courage, and half an hour later was in another position, pounding at the enemy.

At nightfall on Wednesday the position of Waelhem Fort was critical. All supporting artillery was withdrawn to a position on the right at Rumpst, and the fort kept silence for a time. By this means the enemy's fire was withdrawn from the fort, whilst desperate efforts were made to put it again into full fighting trim. The night was marked by an attempt to advance on the part of the enemy with some infantry force. The attempt was repulsed all along the Line. In the field so far the Belgians had proved their superiority. But as a measure of precaution, provisional arrangements were made that night for the removal of the seat of Government to Ostend.

Early on Thursday morning, October 1st, a Zeppelin entered into the combat, making an attempt to bombard the northern forts. The attempt was a ridiculous failure, and not a pennyworth of damage was done, though one bomb fell near Fort Oeleghem. The same morning Fort Wessel succeeded in punishing heavily an attempted German advance.

There was by this time almost a complete evacuation by the civil population of the area under fire. At least fifty thousand refugees must have been poured out on the roads from the various towns and villages. In the evening at five precisely the German guns, turning from Lierre Fort, devoted some shells to Lierre town, and set most of the remainder of the population there, who had braved out the first slight bombardment, to flight. In the evening, about six, the Germans pushed infantry forward with field artillery against the Belgian positions in front of Lierre, Duffel, and Termonde. At Lierre and Termonde the attacks were repulsed. At Duffel the weak point of the infantry was found, and there was a retirement in that quarter.

This in itself was not actually very serious. It was an incident of a battle on a wide front which might easily have been retrieved. But its effect was bad, in that it suggested to divisional commanders that at critical moments some of the infantry was not to be relied upon thoroughly.

Among the citizens of Antwerp it was strongly felt also, for the failure of the water supply gave them gloomy forebodings. (Up to this stage confidence had been general, and it had been apparently justified by the position of affairs.)

Those who before had concluded that the Germans had no valid reason for wasting effort in attacking Antwerp, began now to argue that if Germany had to take up a defensive position along the line of the Meuse and the Rhine, Antwerp would be of great value on the flank as a safe victualling base, defended against attack by the neutral waters of Holland. Still the position was not desperate.

Early on Friday morning I visited Lierre. The town was being bombarded heavily. The position at the fort was good, and there was rejoicing at the defeat of the German attack the previous evening with heavy loss. The bombardment of the town was doing some material damage, but was causing little loss of life, as the town was almost deserted. Going next to a position near Waelhem Fort, it could be seen that the Belgians were holding

THE AGONY OF BELGIUM

their own well. Their field artillery was working most pluckily, and cooperating most effectually with the heavy guns, and the infantry, which was strongly entrenched, was suffering no loss.

A good general impression of the battle in this section of the front up to this point could be gained from the experiences of the artillery of the Fourth Brigade. Commandant Verheyden, a citizen of Louvain, commanding the 8th Battery, narrated to me their movements since Wednesday, when the German bombardment developed strongly. The big shells of the Germans, his officers and men frankly admitted, were at first a little terrifying. They made enormous pits in the ground when they struck, and came through the air with the roar of an express train. In time the men got to laugh at them.

They distinguished between the smaller howitzer shells and the 28-centimetre shells, calling the first trams, the second *trains rapides*, and each big gun was distinguished with a name and its shells noted as express trains from Willebroeck or Heyndonck, or some other place.

This was the battery which had an anxious time when, on Wednesday afternoon, a German shell destroyed the waterworks. Since the action commenced the gunners of this battery had had eighty-four hours' work and sixteen hours' sleep.

It was cheerful and confident on Friday morning, and fired one special round of rapid fire against the enemy out of compliment to me.

But even at that moment the crisis in the fate of Antwerp had come: Fort Waelhem, the southern salient of the position, had fallen. After the fall of Catherine-St. Wavre, Fort Waelhem had met the chief brunt of the German attack. When some of the cupolas were damaged, and it was evident that fire would have to be reduced, Commandant De Wit offered to the men that those who were most fatigued by the long hours of incessant fighting should withdraw from the fort, as only a smaller garrison was now necessary. But the men almost unanimously refused to go back, and it was necessary for the Commandant to give direct orders to some to retire. Though wounded, Commandant De Wit continued to fight at the fort, announcing that he would never leave whilst it was possible to fire another shot at the Germans.

But on Friday morning as I was with the Sixth Field Battery, the

German big shells began to fall like rain on Waelhem. They first destroyed the bridge which constituted the fortress garrison's line of retreat and then smashed the remaining cupolas. As the shells worked havoc in the fort the garrison fixed a ladder across the moat and by this began to retreat. I encountered several of them as they came out of the fort, haggard, weary, smoke-grimed, angry with themselves that they had left even at that last moment. But they had no reason to be ashamed. They had done nobly. The weight of metal was against them. In spite of the silencing of Waelhem the field guns in that sector continued their vigorous fire. I remained with the field batteries for an hour after the end of Waelhem, and was inspired by the confidence of the officers to feel that all was not over with Antwerp yet, and that though the forts might go, whilst there were such bricks of men the city had a wall of security.

At noon on Friday, despite the facts that the Government had arranged to move to Ostend and that a sector of the outer line of forts was destroyed, l was able still to feel a little confident. The afternoon was more depressing. Penetrating to Duffel, the infantry who had retreated were encountered straggling to the rear. But at Lierre, to which town I passed in front of the Belgian line fronting the River Nethe, the aspect of affairs was more cheerful. Returning to Antwerp at six, it seemed reasonable then to hope that on the second line of forts a successful stand could be made. But optimism was discountenanced by seeing a proclamation posted up reminding citizens of their duties and responsibilities towards an enemy's force on entering a town. It seemed clear that the authorities had reason to entertain at least the possibility of a German entry into Antwerp.

Leaving the City at eight, I went out again to the outer line of forts. Under a clear and brilliant night Antwerp and the surrounding country rested calm and beautiful, as if no ugly spirit of war and devastation had ever existed. Not a gun could be heard. Both camps slept in peace, and even the sentries seemed to have an air of quiet and rest. Up to midnight this peace was unbroken. Coming back to the city, I was told, in confidence, that surrender had been decided upon.

CHAPTER IX

ANTWERP FALLS

ON the morning of Saturday, October 3rd, Antwerp, with a road open to the enemy along a great sector of the ring of fortresses, was resigned to her fate. From Fort de Liezel to Fort de Broecken the line of defences was broken, and the safety of the city depended on the infantry holding the line of the Rivers Rupel and Nethe. The Belgian field artillery, for all its gallantry, could not stand out against the heavier and far more numerous field batteries of the Germans.

I counted on a surrender that morning. Instead came news that British help was arriving, and so great was the power of the British name in Belgium, that at once all plucked up hope. Around the Belgian lines the word went round, and the soldiers faced the German fire with new courage.

The events of the siege and fall of the city may now most conveniently be recorded in diary form.

Saturday, October 3rd. – The gloom which reigned yesterday has been dissipated. British aid has come, and the word goes round that Antwerp will be saved. A wave of almost fantastic confidence runs over the city. There are cheering crowds in the streets. Outside on the banks of the Nethe the battle goes on, and refugees still press into the city, but they are as a little drop of sorrow in a great flood of joy and hope. The preparations for the departure of the Government are suspended. Everywhere the word passes that the King and Queen are still in the city, and that the situation is saved.

As if to respond to this flow of hope the alternative water supply actually makes its appearance. There is a little trickle of water through the pipes, not enough for the drainage service, and very brackish. But still water.

Sunday, October 4th. – Cheerfulness continues. The churches are crowded all day, and the prayers are of thankfulness as well as of intercession. A lull in the German attack is taken to be of good augury.

The first of the British forces-Royal Marines-have actually arrived, and at once take the trenches in the hottest corner of the defence position at Lierre. They had travelled all night, but were eager to be at the Germans at once. It is heartening to see the way in which the men chum up with the Belgians, who looked at them with an exaggerated respect.

Very tough fighters these first of the British Forces were, and their work to-night is one of the bright incidents of the siege. They hold their trenches under a galling artillery fire, which is so accurately directed as to give the clearest proof that spies for the Germans had indicated the position of trenches and Maxim stations. A long night of punishment has only one relief, when the German infantry ventures out into the open as if to make an assault. I believe that hardly one German who left his trenches got back in safety, so good was our fire poured into them.

The issue of the battle at this stage is to hold the Nethe River-little more than a canal in width. A non-commissioned officer said to me early in the evening: "There is not going to be a German across that water if I know it." That was the spirit of the defence. It surprises the German considerably evidently; but he is committed so deeply to the attack at this point that he cannot radically change his plan; he has to hammer at Lierre, and the British have to bear the brunt of the attack.

Why the attack had to develop at this point will be clear from the map. Fort Waelhem was the southern salient of the fortified position, and held the key to the direct road to Antwerp. Flank attacks on its west were prohibited by the great width of the Rivers Rupel and Scheldt; on the east of Lierre by a tangle of waterways. Between Waelhem and Lierre was the road with least water obstacles for the passage of big guns. At Waelhem some marshy ground subject to inundation was a natural barrier.

At Duffel, to the east, the way was fairly easy; at Lierre, more to the east, it was most easy.

The City Council has met and passed a resolution consistent with the indomitable spirit of the Belgians.

The resolution urges the Military Governor to act in the best defence of the city, without consideration for any property interests, and promises him the support of the inhabitants to the end.

Monday, October 5th. – The outer suburbs begin to suffer from shell-fire, and this causes some disquiet. But confidence is still the general feeling. People in the street say that it is true that Antwerp may be bombarded.

But that can be endured since the final deliverance is so close at hand. Citizens strengthen their cellars and lay in stocks of food "to see the bombardment through."

The Nethe is held; and further British reinforcements have now arrived, and there seems reason for hope.

Monday night. – The event has proved that the powerful aid which might have been sufficient earlier was not sufficient now, when a section of the forts was already silenced, and the Germans had been able to bring up and establish extraordinarily strong artillery forces on their side of the river. Our infantry was shelled to-night savagely and constantly, without having artillery at its back powerful enough to reply. It had the hardest of all tasks for a force – to stand gruelling punishment without being able to see its enemy. After their lesson of Sunday the German infantry did not dare to come out towards the British trenches. They left the work to the artillery. Fagged-out, tormented, our men might have been excused if they had lost spirit.

But they have not done so, and stick it out with a courage worthy of all praise. The misfortune of the night was not due to any lack either on their part or that of the Belgians.

A ruse of war, a characteristically German ruse (though lawful enough), was the actual cause. At the Duffel position the trenches were held by a regiment of Belgian chasseurs. Late at night the sentries saw approaching them from along the river-side men whom they thought were English soldiers, and who called out *"Amis"* when challenged. The Colonel of the regiment himself saw them go up as if to speak to the sentries, and then found himself gagged and saw the two sentries strangled. The Germans then rushed in on the men, who were mostly asleep in their trenches, and more than half destroyed the regiment. Of two thousand men only eight hundred remained.

The hope which had come with the British has now fled. The Lierre position is outflanked, and can be no longer held. The abandonment of the line of the Nethe is inevitable; and the defenders determine on a stand along the second line of forts.

Tuesday, October 6th – Stern facts have eaten away our confidence. The German circle of fire tightens on the city. The area of devastation spreads. The Cathedral tower flies the red and white flag prescribed by the Geneva Convention for the protection of public monuments in case of the bombardment of a city.

It is stated that the Germans will respect this sign, and that their guns will spare the Cathedral. We listen and we hope, but we do not expect. Whatever there is devilish and desecratory to be done we fear that the Germans will do.

As I am told of the flag, at the Malines Gate there clamours a great horde of fugitives from the villages and outlying suburbs shelled by the Germans. Among them are two young nuns, each pushing a wheelbarrow containing an aged nun. The sight has something of the terribly grotesque as well as of the pitiful, and, seeing, one's mouth is twisted to the risus sardonicus of the dead. The Germans show any compunction, spare anything sacred? Ask of these fugitives!

The crowd is kept back from entry to the city by files of soldiers. Miserable, miserable, they flee to Antwerp as a city of refuge, and from that Antwerp her own citizens are fleeing in terror.

As I see these fugitives in their thousands, thronging the roadside, begging with dumb patience that sternly-necessary orders will be set aside, and that they should be admitted to seek for the safety which they search for in vain, I see in my mind the driving out of the Belgian people from their land from first to last.

For two months now I have stood by and seen this bitter punishment of a people found guilty in the Court of the Kaiser of having been true to a trust and faithful to a bond. I have seen them coming from out of Tirlemont to Louvain for refuge, and turning from Louvain to Brussels, and from Brussels to Malines, and from Malines to the shelter of the Antwerp forts: and now to the city itself. This is the last scene in the long-drawn-out martyrdom of a nation. They have come here to find a foothold, and the foothold is already crumbling away under the fire of the German guns. Pitiful beyond words or tears, only endurable by thinking of the stern requital which must come.

Among the fugitives some have nothing to eat. But in the common misfortune all have become as one family. A child, gnawing at a root hungrily, finds slipped into his hand a portion of the insufficient bread of another. The poor help the poorer. I see a man give his coat to an old man who is cold, pointing to the fact that he has a warm waistcoat and can spare it.

Need I add that these files of soldiers with fixed bayonets do not for very long keep the fugitives outside the city walls? It is, in one sense, desirable, perhaps necessary, that they should do so, for the city wants all its energies for defence. But the Belgian people are too soft-hearted to do a necessary cruelty. After a little while the fugitives pass in: and later, doubtless, pass out again on the north side towards Holland on their Calvary.

In the afternoon the *Matin* announces officially that the position of Antwerp is grave, and that a bombardment of the city is to be expected. Very sadly the bulk of the people set about preparations for departure.

The artillery attack of the Germans this morning has been diffuse. It has seemed to have no fixed objective at all. Heavy shells have been discharged here, there, and everywhere, finding targets in fields and in houses more often than on defended positions. This is a welcome relief after the experience of our troops yesterday, who in some positions found themselves under shell-fire so exact as to indicate with almost positive certainty the presence on the spot of spies sending signals to the enemy.

A much stricter guard is now kept over the battle area to prevent the intrusion of civilians, and today over a great part of the field the German fire was not well directed. It is possible that this is partly the result of the stricter guard.

At nightfall, except for frantic attacks on the Lierre position, the German effort is slight. But at Lierre the fighting is most savage. Our forces, after pushing forward a small detachment across the river, for a time had to retire to their own side. During this attack an instance of personal gallantry should be recorded. Two soldiers swam across the river with their wounded sergeant. Unhappily he died after reaching our lines.

"Never before have I seen such fierce fighting," said one of the combatants, describing the engagement. Surveying the position from a high tower this evening, it was possible to see why the

German attack is concentrated at Lierre, for at that point the water defences are less formidable.

It is a clear, cold night. The infantry battle is likely to continue. During the evening I visit Boom, which was bombarded last week. The bombardment killed nine of the civil population and inflicted some slight damage. The Civic Guard of the town has pluckily stood to its post, and last night sallied out and repulsed a German attempt to establish a mitrailleuse station on the Belgian side of the river.

Wednesday, October 7th: Morning – All night Antwerp has been surrounded with noisy flame. The Nethe has been held as only soldiers of the best could hold it. But the loss of life has been woeful. It is in artillery force that we are lacking. The result of the night's fighting I cannot yet clearly know. It is announced that when the bombardment of the city opens, the safest quarters are the north and the north-east. With perhaps a deficient sense of duty I am going out to seek a fairly safe shelter before visiting the line of battle. The bombardment is expected to begin after 10 p.m.

From the suburbs fugitives come in full of tales of terror. If one were to accept hearsay evidence it would be certain that there are a million Germans within a mile of Antwerp: that all outlying places are in flames. But truly it is not as bad as that. We have the fighting chance left and a proclamation of the Governor breathes courage and resolution. It should be set up in a high place in witness to the courage of the Belgians:

"J'ai l'honneur de porter à la connaissance de la population que le bombardement de l'agglomération d'Anvers et des environs est imminent.

"Il est bien entendu que la menace ou l'exécution du bombardement n'auront aucune influence sur la durée de la résistance qui sera conduite jusqu'à la dernière extrémité.

"Les personnes qui veulent se soustraire aux effets du dit bombardement sont priées de se retirer dans le plus bref délai, dans la direction du Nord ou du Nord-Est."

Citizens who wish to escape the dangers of a bombardment rush from the town at every gate except those fronting the line

107

of fire. At the riverside, boat after boat loads with refugees. Clamouring crowds fill the railway stations. Along the roads streams of pedestrians pushing little hand-carts, dragging along bundles, leading dogs, goats, cows, pigs, pass for the coast or for the Holland frontier.

I, who have seen the Belgian nation driven back, little by little, until this, its last stronghold, was reached, feel again all the woe and horror of the last two months. The first stream of fugitives from Tirlemont comes back to my sight clearly, vividly. They take the head of the terrible procession, and after them come the fugitives from Louvain, from Brussels, from Aerschot, from Termonde, from Alost, from Boom, from all the quarters of Belgium. A nation goes out in flight, leaving of its numbers many murdered, of its homes and shrines many burned and devastated.

Not all the civilians are in flight. I hear on many sides of instances of civil courage. At a big commercial house two of the employees will stay and have made a bomb-proof shelter.

A fine note of courage is struck in the *Matin* this morning, which points out that the fate of Antwerp depends upon the grand battle of the Aisne, and it adds:

> "It is this reason which has decided England to make the powerful effort which we all admire to reinforce its contingent in France. For only fresh troops, sufficiently trained and skilled in musketry, can have a decisive result on the battle front there."

It is splendid to note that at this terrible moment of her destiny Belgium, speaking through her press, takes the large view, sees the danger to Europe rather than the misery of Antwerp, and applauds the decision which will leave Antwerp to its fate because it seems the wisest decision for the common cause. Belgium, between August 2nd and October 7th, has not been tortured either out of her resolution or her clear sight.

The Government has withdrawn to St.Nicholas across the Scheldt on the road to Ghent, in the hope that though Antwerp should fall another stand may be possible there.

I have found what seems a reasonably safe hotel. The authorities suggested cellars and referred to the north and north-east parts of the city as the safest quarters. I explored those parts and found them wanting in any good accommodation and far from the centre of things; and one resolution is firm in my mind-not to allow any German terror to drive me to living in a cellar.

The Hôtels Métropôle and Wagner are suggested as fairly safe ones. I rule out the "Métropôle" at once as having two towers-fine marks for gun-layers-and facing the broad, open Place de Meir with a direct southerly outlook into the very mouth of the German big guns. The Hôtel Wagner is better. It is behind the great Flemish Opera House and faces north on to a little square planted with trees. The German guns firing from the south would have to batter down the Opera House before reaching the "Wagner." Nor could a plunging shell "find" the "Wagner" with any possible trajectory, for it is lower than the Opera House. Shells clearing the hotel and bursting on the square would be smothered in all likelihood among the grass and trees.

The event proved the wisdom of the choice. I slept (for some hours) through both nights of the bombardment on the second floor with open windows, taking only the precaution of placing a pillow as a screen for my head against remotely possible splinters. One shell burst in the square, and did no damage except to smash the windows next door and a glass in my room with the force of the air-currents. When out exploring the streets amid tumbling houses it was singularly comforting to know that there was a fairly secure retreat for an occasional rest.

Wednesday evening.-This afternoon official advice is given to the population regarding safety during the bombardment.

People are advised not to show themselves in the streets, to betake themselves to vaulted cellars, to cover over the street gratings of the cellars with mattresses or sacks of earth, to keep on each floor some vessels of water with which to put out fire (there is little or no water, but otherwise the advice is good). Those of the population who go out of the city into the country are urged to take with them food and blankets. All are advised to cut off the gas, and candles are recommended as the safest illuminant. As an additional precaution the city's gasometers are emptied.

The lions, the tigers, the other great animals and the serpents in the magnificent Zoo have been destroyed. The Zoo is near the railway station, and it is feared that it might be damaged and the beasts break loose.

Merciful men go about the streets shooting the homeless dogs. One of the minor miseries of the great exodus from Antwerp is that hundreds of dogs have lost their masters and wander about the streets pitifully seeking some human friendship. With the wolves at the gate it is best that the dogs should die.

All the hospitals are being emptied. The staffs of the Legations and of most of the Consulates depart.

All who can do so follow their example. There is hardly a carriage of any kind left in the city. People wait in long files for a chance to get on a boat going down the river towards safety, and after waiting sometimes for as long as twelve hours are turned away disappointed. These people who are thus disappointed besiege one with inquiries as to whether there is any danger. Will the Germans come? Will the city be set on fire? Will all be massacred?

The telegraph offices close in the afternoon even for the État-Major. The newspapers cease publication. Civic life has ceased. Over the gratings of the cellars the sprinkled earth suggests that here are the freshly-made tombs of homes. In the evening the remainder of the population wanders through the streets uneasily, seeking comfort and reassurance.

I am told of another characteristic Germanism. A Taube has come over the city and has scattered proclamations telling the population that the Germans are their real friends, and urging them to surrender and not fight longer "for Russian tyranny." Then, I am told, the Taube dropped bombs, one of which killed a maidservant. But investigation shows that whilst the account of the proclamations is correct the "bomb" proves to have been a shell discharged at the aeroplane by one of our forts and unhappily killing a passer-by. The truth is a little disappointing! The other would have been so German-first the proclamation and then the bomb.

The Civic Guard has been disarmed and freed from duty.

There is one slender chance left: if the British naval guns, which are said to have arrived, can come into position quickly enough to give effective support to the Belgian garrison and the British Marines, Antwerp may be snatched out of the jaws of death.

The fighting going on along our line is rather slaughter than fighting now, as the German artillery is so overwhelming. This afternoon it is possible to get but a very little distance out of the actual city limits. All the outer suburbs are under shell-fire. The ring of German fire clamps closer around the city.

Coming back to the city at 4 p.m., I find a Taube surveying the city like a carrion crow from the sky. The slaughter of our men goes on and the hospitals are full; the dead in the trenches are many. The soldiers stick to it and pray for the guns which are going to save the situation.

An unhappy feature of the fighting is that clearly, unmistakably, the German gunners are advised from our field of battle. Our General Staff comes under shell-fire whatever position it takes up. The position of our trenches is known with exact accuracy as soon as they are occupied.

Thursday, October 8th. – The bombardment of the city proper actually commenced at 1 a.m. with the great 28-centimetre guns. On the explosion of the first of these shells, in the southern quarter, all Antwerp seems to be shaken by the shattering concussion. The people pour out into the streets, and a hurried flight on foot towards the Holland frontier begins. Past the Avenue de Commerce on the northern road an endless procession goes. The night is clear and moonlit, and the flames from burning houses in the suburbs give further light. Barely is there to be seen a vehicle of any kind in the procession. These fugitives are mostly the poor, who to the last moment have held to the hope that the bombardment would not come.

Some press forward with wild haste, turning back now and again to see the terror behind. Most plod on quietly, almost listlessly. These people have suffered so much as to have lost all sensation. Occasionally a woman shrieks, or a child wails. But in the main the procession keeps an awful and severe silence. Overhead the shells scream exultantly as they fly to their work. When one falls the whole earth appears to tremble at the roar, and a house pours out into the street or a pavement bursts into eruption.

Most of the shells find their way into houses. Rarely is a fugitive-crowded street struck, and the loss of life seems to be small, though many deaths probably are hidden in the ruins of the houses.

The shells come in clusters of six very methodically into one particular quarter, and the big guns are then deflected a little to attack another quarter. Only the southern sections of the city are reached in this first bombardment. Evidently the gun-layers are setting their sights by the church spires, for around each spire is an area of havoc.

I am told the bombardment was officially timed for 10 p.m., according to the German notice. It was a subtle bit of Germanism to delay the blow for three hours, striking at the time when human courage is at its ebb-tide.

I speculate on the thoughts of those gunners out there five, six, perhaps eight miles away. Do they, as they lay their guns, think at all of what home the shells will strike, speculate on what men, women or children will be killed? They are not firing at forts now, nor at camps, but at city streets where the helpless non-combatants live in frail houses. Whatever they think, they do their work with cruel precision.

I had resolved when the first of the shells came not to go out into the streets that night. It might be a long task, this siege and bombardment, and I had had but two hours' sleep. But turning back to rest, I was made uneasy by an overpowering smell of kerosene. The air was permeated with it. Was this some new machine of atrocity that the Germans had designed-a shell to scatter petrol as a harbinger to incendiary shells? The question drove me out into the streets, and a sentry near the old headquarters of the État-Major, sniffing the air, said certainly the Germans were preparing to burn the city. The overpowering odour was everywhere, overcoming altogether the reek from the city drainage channels, stopped now for a week by the want of water.

Going to the River Scheldt I found that the cause of the odour was less alarming. The Belgian authorities had let flow all the oil and petrol from the great stores at Hoboken. In the light of the moon and of the reflection in the sky of the fires in the suburbs a river of oil flows down green and ghastly. An incendiary shell there now would wrap all the quays in flames and destroy the two bridges of boats which are the only means of communication left between the city and Ghent. But it does not come.

After two hours the bombardment slackens a little and then

is resumed with new intensity at 5 a.m. At six I cycle along the Chaussée de Malines, the main road leading to the Malines Gate. Right and left of the road the quarter is being rent and shattered. Near here are placed the little villas of the *bourgeois* and also the great houses of the German magnates who used to batten on Antwerp. Several of these houses are torn open and strewn into the street.

Fugitives stream along the road, seeking safety. Some have waited to gather up a few household goods; cash-boxes can be recognized in many hands. Others have come out in the last moment of panic without anything. Little children, urged on by their parents, turn back as they hear the scream of a coming shell, half in terror, half in curiosity. From some houses sick and wounded are carried on stretchers. The noise of the bombardment is infernal, the air torn constantly by the scream of the passing shell and then pounded and battered by its gigantic explosion.

Anxious to penetrate through to Vieux Dieu (Oude God), which is the centre of the fighting, I dodge my way along the Chaussée de Malines towards the Malines Gate, on the way calling in at a sheltered square where a motor supply detachment had taken refuge. To pass the Malines Gate, however, is impossible at this moment. Literally the air is full of flying bricks. Struck in the shoulder lightly by one, I take it as a warning tap from a friendly hand and turn back to a corner of the city where the shells are not so thick.

On the banks of the Scheldt the two bridges of boats are packed densely with fugitives. At the approaches there are inextricable tangles of motors, horse carriages, hand-carts, cyclists, foot-passengers. It is a tangle of fear, of haste, of reckless urging. Motor-cars, with their occupants weeping, carts with their peasants or little traders stoical, foot-passengers (who seem the most cheerful), jostle and push and clamour for the way; and their haste prevents progress towards the narrow bridge, along which traffic must crawl. The traffic chokes itself with its own hurry and dread. If the German shells should find this quarter now thousands of lives would be lost. But Heaven is kind, and the struggling mass slowly, oh! so slowly, percolates through the narrow passage to the other shore which is nearer to safety.

A Civic Guard, holding to his post, talks to me a little scornfully:

"They have fear, these people. And why have fear? The English are holding all the line: there is no reason to fear. We are safe with them."

I tried to be a little deprecatory, but he was firm.

"The English never go away," he repeats.

I hope he will prove right. But seeing our wounded coming back from the front, all with the same cry for "the guns," I cannot be too confident.

Last night fighting was more desperate than ever all along the line. Our men-Belgians and British-are fighting gallantly, but there is still the inferiority in artillery. We are outnumbered ten to one in gun power, and, counting the actual effectives on our side, five to one in numbers. Since the Germans have committed themselves so strongly to the attack they have brought up reinforcements. A significant fact is that many of the German dead are in civil uniforms. This our men have found when they have won back a little *terrain*. I cannot say whether it is that the Germans are using now reserves without uniforms or whether it is the case, as at Alost, that they put Belgian civilians in the fighting line. But our men say that these German dead in civilian attire have rifles. At Alost the civilian Belgian dead were unarmed.

In the afternoon I go out on a cycle to explore the northern portion of the city towards the Breda Gate, which I had marked out as the line of retreat when the Germans came. The northern part of the city had been recommended by the authorities as the safest from shells. It is a poor industrial quarter, very closely packed. Surprised, I find that it is under very heavy shell-fire, and there is some serious loss of life because very many of the people had stayed here. Laying their guns on two prominent church steeples, the Germans are pouring high-explosive shell into this quarter. The poor little houses give no resistance at all, and the shells pass through them from street to street.

It is difficult to get past the heaps of ruins, and I have to carry the cycle most of the way, because of the broken glass that is everywhere. Some people are in flight; others stand or squat outside their houses in passive despair. From one house of two storeys as it collapses a woman's body falls; if she uttered a shriek it is drowned in the roar of the explosion. I hear of many dead and wounded. Some brave ambulance men are taking the wounded away.

Back to the Scheldt in the afternoon: the rush across the river continues. Traversing the Place de Meir on the safety side-that protected by the southern row of buildings- the opposite side is being struck by shells, which pass through their fronts and smash up at the back. The quarter which received the first Zeppelin bomb is struck by one shell and its ruined house collapses utterly. There seems to be no loss of life here, for no inhabitants are left. A fire starts in the Marché des Souliers, almost opposite the Hôtel St. Antoine. From the Scheldt great clouds of smoke arise. Going there, I find that the oil tanks-the majority empty or nearly empty – are aflame, and bits of burning *débris* are floating down the stream, threatening the bridges of boats.

Going to see if the Cathedral were still safe, I have two narrow escapes from shells, and feel that enough exploration has been done for the afternoon and go to my retreat at the Hôtel Wagner.

I go out again to explore a house with bombproof cellars and a good stock of wine and provisions, quarters in which are offered by a friend. I am not at all inclined to change, as the place indicated, between the railway and the Chausée de Malines, is right in the line of fire, but reluctantly decide to go and see. My friend is inclined to take the shells lightly and is a little amused at my precautions of running across unsheltered streets and dodging under doorways when a near shriek tells that a shell is coming. Soon he is fully converted. At a spot which we had passed a minute before a house is thrown out into the street with a roar and a rattle. On our way we see five houses in all smashed up. We persevere to the house, explore it, and come back, content not to move.

Evening falls, and I climb up to the roof of the Hôtel Wagner and overlook almost the whole city, the view partly cut off in only one direction by the Flemish Opera House, which is five feet higher than the hotel.

The spectacle is one of grandeur as well as of horror. Satan, it would seem, has set up his throne over the city, and in infernal pomp takes the homage of the Powers of Darkness. The night-out from the area of the city – I know, is clear, cold, absolutely still, bright with the silver radiance of the moon. Over Antwerp a great blanket of smoke shuts out the moon, the stars, the clean sweet air of Heaven, the gracious coolth; and it is as if the city had descended into Hell. It is enveloped in a dank, hot mist. From the burning oil tanks three round pillars of smoke ascend and support the black pall. The fires in the suburbs and in the Marché des Souliers give to the southern edge of this cloud of naphtha-smoke a lining which is not red and not yellow, but an unearthly colour somewhat like that of chlorine fumes.

Against this hideous lining of a hideous cloud the spires, minarets, chimneys, gable corners of the city, dance a dance of fiends. The Cathedral tower, lit up from its base by a fire near, alone stands out from this devils' phantasmagoria and seems clean, wholesome, a citadel of hope.

Hope seems an absurd word, but going into the streets again I penetrate to the cellar of a Red Cross official, and he, strangely enough, speaks of hope. "Antwerp will be bombarded for five days, and then the Germans will be defeated." He is a mere lad, who knows nothing, but I find comfort in talking to him.

But going out into the streets again I find Belgian and British troops in retreat across the Scheldt. Clearly all is over. A Belgian staff officer explains to me the formidable nature of the task set to the defenders:

"We were outclassed in artillery from the first. In consequence the Germans were able to destroy a section of the outer forts and with them some of the confidence of our men. When the British aid arrived the position was almost hopeless. Without that aid surrender was inevitable. With it we had only a gambler's chance. The German plan of attack was to harass our men day and night with artillery, and only bring up their infantry at the last moment. It came fresh against wearied and outnumbered men."

There is no need to recount the details hour by hour of a story always the same. The German superiority in guns was overwhelming. Our troops held their ground with marvellous tenacity, but finally had to yield little by little. As the circle of defence grew narrower they got some of their own back from the Germans. Ground was lost and won back again, but ultimately it was a question of extrication. Throughout, the troubles of the Staff were added to by the fact that the Germans were kept advised by spies on the actual battle-ground of our positions.

Wherever the General Staff established itself it found itself at once under murderous shell-fire.

At the last the Belgian General nobly takes on the responsibility for his army of acting as rear-guard.

Friday, October 9th. Throughout last night the few who remained in Antwerp had every prompting to terror and agonizing doubt. The flames of the burning oil tanks enveloped the city in a dark pall of green-black smoke, to which the flames of burning houses gave a lining of lurid yellow. Through this pall came shrieking the great shells of the 28-centimetre guns, each one smashing one or more houses, and crashing like a thunderbolt as it sent buildings actually pouring into the streets. Beneath the pall of smoke, along the ways of the shattered city, went the tumbrils and hurrying ranks of a retiring army.

Many of the people of Antwerp had resolved to withstand the bombardment of the city as the last penalty they would have to pay before the vindication of their national cause: and were content to stay, burrowing among its ruins, so long as the Germans could be kept out. To them the retreat of the defending army was the last blow of Fate. They abandoned the cellars and retreats which they had prepared and provisioned and set out in flight.

It was the last and most pitiful exodus, for these were the elect of the citizens, the brave men and their brave wives who were for Antwerp whilst the city had one building left to fly a flag. Through the streets they passed, north and east, to the Dutch frontier, or towards the quays, some meeting their death as they went from the bombardment which went pitilessly on, seeking, it seemed, in particular at this stage to search the northern roads leading towards Holland.

As the fugitives passed they gave way here and there for the retreating troops, and, one may think, took some grain of comfort to their brave hearts in the fact that most of these troops passed towards the Scheldt bridges and therefore towards the last of Belgian territory unoccupied by the enemy.

On Friday morning at six, the bombardment slackened for a little. Going to some officers' quarters in the vaults under the Central Railway Station, I found them deserted. Through a mile almost of the great subterranean passages I tramped, seeking an officer, a sentry, a sign of hope. As gallery after gallery of the vaults proved to be empty the sense of abandonment gave a chill foreboding which some hairbreadth escapes from shell fragments had not given.

This truly was the abomination of desolation.

A railway porter outside, stolid, apathetic, miserable, told me that all the soldiers had gone and the Germans would be in soon. How soon? In half an hour, he had heard; and he stood there listlessly and waited.

A hospital had promised a chance of escape on its ship for the three of us – two correspondents and a woman author – who had stayed on. I went to the hospital seeking this lifeline, before going on to the Hôtel de Ville for the definite news of the surrender. The hospital had gone. All around it the shell-fire of the night had wrought ruin-fire directed probably at the railway station. As I stood outside a shell struck a brick house in the street, and with a crashing roar the house went up into the air as a red cloud and came raining down in bricks and mortar.

That shell, strangely enough, was a little comforting. It argued that the German Army would not be actually in the city, or else the bombardment would have ceased altogether.

On a cycle I set out to explore the night's devastation. It had been very serious. The centre of the city chiefly had been attacked, and all round the Central Railway Station, the Cathedral, and the Royal Palace, along the Place de Meir, and at the back of that street, were houses altogether ruined and great pits in the streets from which had been vomited up, as from a volcano, paving stones and shell splinters, which smashed in the fronts of the houses they struck.

Coming from an examination of the Cathedral, undamaged, but with the ruins of a house spread as a threat at its very door, I encountered two British marines who had lost their regiment and their way and asked the road to safety. I took them along to the bank of the Scheldt, learning as I went their story of the night.

Nearing the Scheldt, heavy firing was heard from light artillery. We pushed on quickly. The second bridge of boats had been set on fire in two places, and our artillery was engaged in smashing the bridge in other places. The other bridge, higher up the river, of more recent construction, had been destroyed by the Belgians during the night. It was now half-past seven on Friday morning. All line of retreat towards Ostend was cut off. The bombardment at this time was not severe, about one heavy shell a minute.

Going back to the Place de Meir, I noticed that the one portion of the city actually set on fire by the German shells (a group of shops in the Marché des Souliers, near the Hôtel St. Antoine, where the Legations were sheltered) was burning itself out. There was no wind and therefore this fire did not spread. It had started on Thursday evening, and up to this point had been left to its own will. Now a small band of firemen were trying to pull down the tottering walls of the shops. It was brave work at such a time. In the Place de Meir I encountered again a group of British marines and the one journalist colleague who was staying with Antwerp to the last. We march with the marines to the Scheldt, and show them the nearest way to Holland, since it is better to be a prisoner in Holland than in Germany.

Some sensational stories written by "eye-witnesses" who were a frontier or so away have described the "burning" of Antwerp. It was not burned. The oil tanks at Hoboken were set on fire after the bulk of the oil had been run into the Scheldt: three shops at one corner near the Hôtel St. Antoine were burned out, and one other shop near the Hôtel de Ville was set slightly on fire in the last hour of the bombardment. In the suburbs many houses were burned. The destruction of property by high-explosive shells was huge. But clearly no incendiary shells were used. Since the town was without water, and until Friday morning without fire-fighters, any general employment of incendiary shells would have caused its entire destruction.

At eight o'clock at the Hôtel de Ville it was clear that something was afoot. A motor-car was drawn up along the one side of it sheltered somewhat from shell fire, and officials passed to and fro. The following proclamation, dated October 7th, had been just posted up announcing the departure of the Government:

"After long hesitations and vain attempts to secure a victory on other fields of battle the German Army has pursued for a month now the siege of the fortified position of Antwerp. In these circumstances the Government has a duty not only to maintain the communications with all parts of the country not occupied by the enemy, but to place safe from all risk the liberty of its deliberations and of its actions, the continuity of its relations with the guaranteeing Powers and with the other nations who accord to our valiant country their sympathies and good wishes.

"Sacrificing itself to imperious obligations, of which all patriots will measure the importance, the Government has decided to transfer itself to another point of the national territory. It quits Antwerp with a grateful memory of its generous hospitality and takes pleasure in proclaiming that, faithful to its high national mission, this noble city has for almost two months assured to the Government a perfect tranquillity in carrying on all its public functions.

"After as before its departure, the Army will oppose to the enemy the most obstinate resistance. The Government has the certainty that the valiant population of Antwerp will in its turn support with stoicism our common trials with the same sentiment of patriotism as our other cities and our more humble villages, and will await with an unbroken confidence the approaching hour of deliverance and reparation."

Either from inadvertence, or from a desire to postpone publication of what might be a prompting to panic, this proclamation was only now given out. Its pathos was heightened by the fact that it was read – or disregarded – by the group of twelve people around the Hôtel de Ville, when plainly the last scene of surrender had come.

At 8.30 the Burgomaster, with three of his Sheriffs, entered the motor-car, to go in search of General von Bessere, the German Commander in charge of the attack. The Burgomaster bore himself with a simple and touching dignity. He stated what was his mission, and then his sorrow plainly begged to be spared questions.

The Burgomaster had scarcely left the square in front of the Hôtel de Ville when a savage bombardment of the spot began. That building and the Cathedral – both of which the Germans had promised to spare-were most clearly aimed at. Twelve shells fell within six minutes over an area of fifty square yards.

The very air seemed torn and shattered by them as houses went up into dust and paving stones spouted up into the air. One shell fell on the pavement within ten yards of the south-eastern corner of the Hôtel de Ville, smashed all the windows there, wrecked the front of the Municipal offices at the back, and sent a flood of *débris* sweeping up the street. Another wrecked a shop on the right-hand side of the square. Another smashed a shop at the opposite corner and its roof caught fire. Two more fell at the back of that shop, very, very close to the Cathedral. The path of the others I could not trace, for the air was dark with fumes and dust.

I was sheltering under the lee of the Hôtel de Ville in front of the statue of Brabo. A municipal servant came to the window of the basement to warn me of the danger of staying there. As I pleaded that it was necessary to stay, he opened a door and admitted me to the basement, from which one could see fairly well, and yet have the shelter of iron bars from flying fragments. In the cellars behind were sheltering all the Consular representatives remaining in the city, and the Mexican Consul very civilly made me welcome. He had stood to his post of duty and was awaiting the return of the Burgomaster with the German authorities to present himself. He is very urgent that I should go at once towards the Dutch frontier as he thinks it likely that the Germans will promptly seize all the gates leading out of the city; and he knows what would be the fate of an English journalist caught in the city.

But it is necessary to wait for the last phase of the last scene.

The scene is set with all appropriateness for this tragedy, which marks another painful stage in the Calvary of an heroic little people being trodden under foot because they stood for honour and good faith. Above, the halls of the splendid city palace, opulent in marble and oak carving and gilding, splendid with the glowing work of Leys and Lagye illustrating the glories of Antwerp of the sixteenth century, await the invader. Beneath, a few faithful servants of the city cower in the cellars, thinking, doubtless, of their Burgomaster out in the rain of shells, and await his word to perform their last sad duties. Outside, the statue of Brabo stands amid a wilderness of bricks, masonry, glass, fragments of shells, torn bits of buildings, riven paving stones.

And over all the beautiful tower of the Cathedral, standing like a sentinel poplar over the Scheldt, seems to mourn and droop.

It is impossible to see and to think over it in the stifling air of the cellar. I feel a suffocation, a tightening of the heart, a sickness of the soul, and must go out to the fresh air, at whatever risk of shells.

The bombardment is not so heavy, and there is shown a last instance of the fine courage of the Belgians. (Often they have lacked experience, but never courage, these two dreadful months.) A little group of firemen have set to work to quench the fire in the shop opposite. Two of them are working on the roof, and they call for "Water, water." A peasant woman brings two buckets from the back of the Hôtel de Ville, and then hesitates and sets them down short of that shell-swept street. For very shame's sake, seeing those two men on the roof, I have to go and take up the buckets. My colleague calls out that he will take one, but two are as easy to carry as one, and he waits for the next two, which, fortunately, are not necessary. The fire is quenched. It threatened the Cathedral if it had got a hold.

We wait, my colleague* and I. The shell fire slackens, and we venture down to the Scheldt to see the burning bridge, and then, most grateful wonder, down the stream shows a little motor-boat. Up to this we had had two bicycles (one without tyres) as the sole means of escape. The owner of the motor-boat makes terms, and agrees to await until the last.

Back to the Hôtel de Ville to wait, and at 10.30 the bombardment ceases. A quarter of an hour after a message comes from the Burgomaster, and one of the civic staff goes out to post up type-written proclamations which have been ready beforehand.

One, dated October 8th, but now (10.30 a.m., October 9th) first given out, is from Lieutenant-General De Guise, Commandant of Antwerp, warning all ill-intentioned persons from taking advantage of the bombardment and the partial abandonment of the town to do acts of pillage.

The second, dated also October 8th, states that since the Government had left Antwerp, the

Burgomaster took over control with a Commission to assist

---

*Mr. Lucien Arthur Jones of the *Daily Chronicle.*

him, and they would do their best to keep order.

The third asked all citizens to deliver up their arms at the Police Bureau; enjoined on the police a house-to-house canvass to see that this was done; warned citizens against committing any act of violence or enmity towards the Germans; advised those who fled from the town to take with them food and blankets; announced that the civic dignitaries would stay at their posts, and begged all to maintain order and calmness.

At noon a messenger comes that the Germans are entering by the Malines Gate, and five minutes after our motor-boat is making its slow way down the Scheldt, the surface of which is covered with oil and burning *débris* from the destruction of the Hoboken tanks. On either shore is a fringe of refugees fleeing from the Huns towards hospitable Holland.

It is a grey, cold day. The river reeks of petrol, is charred with burning rubbish, shows here and there the dead body of a soldier, is framed on either side with a tattered silhouette of despairing fugitives.

But, looking back, the tower of the Cathedral, intact, beautiful, stands like a sentinel poplar on guard for the Belgian nation, promising that Heaven will soon right the wrongs and miseries of today.

Antwerp, which survived her cruel trials in the fourteenth century, which was not destroyed by the Duke of Alva, nor yet by the horrors of the Furie Espagnoli, which withstood the siege of Alexander Farnese for fourteen months, will forget the humiliation of today and revive its proud history.

CHAPTER X

HOW THE GERMAN FIGHTS

THERE have been published between August and December, 1914, many vivid and popular descriptions of the methods of the German Army in the field. Briefly summarized they have amounted to this: that the German artillery is usually poorly aimed and its ammunition defective: that the German infantry cannot shoot, always advances into action in massed formation, and leaves behind hillocks of slain as it suffers its inevitable defeat.

Comforting as are such accounts, they leave us in a little doubt as to why under these circumstances the German Army is in possession of almost all Belgium, the richest district of France, and a great portion of Poland, in spite of the skilful and gallant French, Russian, British and Belgian armies. I must venture on a description of the German Army methods which will be less obviously "patriotic."

A general impression of German war tactics after some observation in the field left these two points outstanding: (1) The wonderful thoroughness of preparation on the part of the German nation for this war; and (2) the failure of the German nation to assert a superiority over, or even an equality with, its British, French, and Belgian antagonists in unforeseen contingencies calling for individual initiative.

In all that could be provided for by thought beforehand, in all the book-work and routine of war, in the matters of discipline and of equipment, the German force was generally above criticism. In those other things which tell of the character of a race, of its native wit, and its natural courage, the German has often taken second place to the Belgian, the Frenchman, the British man. Constantly, therefore, in considering the German at war, I was moved to astonishing alternations of applause and censure.

But perhaps there is an explanation which will do away with the astonishment. It was impossible that an intelligent and methodical people should devote their whole energies to the perfection of a plan of aggressive war without securing great results; but impossible also that this devotion to a single and inhuman end should not have de-humanized the people somewhat, lowered their general intelligence, injured their spirit of initiative. To train for the defence of one's own country is, I suppose, an almost necessary part of intelligent life. But to submit to a military despotism for the sake of organizing a war of conquest over one's neighbours must spoil the citizen somewhat in drilling the soldier. Germany has profited in the field by the scientific exactness of her war equipment and the blind obedience of her slavishly-drilled people. She has lost in the field by the failure of those people under Circumstances when equipment failed and a "common-sense shift" was called for, when obedience was not sufficient and an individual *élan* and judgment was wanted.

In regard to equipment, the first days of the campaign disclosed how perfected was the German war machine in this regard. The first German dead gave up many secrets. The German soldier was clothed in cloth of a colour which on the average of European days gives a greater degree of invisibility than khaki. This cloth was excellently woven to withstand weather and strain. Each soldier carried in his pocket-knife a little equipment for mending his clothes (as also a little first-aid Red Cross bandage of adhesive plaster). His boots were of wonderfully strong and supple leather, such boots as only civilians in good circumstances can buy. His valise of cowhide, tanned with the hair on, was most ingeniously furnished with straps and removable bolts of white metal for ease of carrying and ease of packing and unpacking. Its contents, disposed in various little cupboards, gave the maximum of food reserve and clothing comforts for the space and weight.

Quite regardless of the value of the soldier's life at the critical moment of an action, the German plan equipped him perfectly at the outset, even with materials to facilitate the work of pillage and incendiarism which had been mapped out for him. The order-books of officers and non-commissioned officers showed the same meticulous devotion to detail. During all the years of preparation the German mind evidently devoted itself with passionate industry to providing for every possible emergency of the soldier's life in the field.

As the equipment was the zenith, the cavalry tactic was the nadir of the German Army. Whether against the Belgian, French, or British cavalry the German cavalry was always inferior. The much-advertised Uhlans might appear from some episodes to have done good, daring work.

But in real fact they were simply shot out from headquarters like stones from a catapult, recklessly, non-intelligently, to raid somewhere, anywhere. With so many of them out they had to blunder on some successes. In the aggregate their record was one of failure. Repeatedly they were trapped and almost exterminated by far inferior forces, and I recall one instance (of many) near Osmael when six Belgian cyclists ambushed twenty-five Uhlans and killed thirteen of them without suffering any loss.

On the march the Uhlans had no skill of scouting. In the first phase of the war the German idea of cavalry on the march in hostile country was for a squadron of twenty-five to precede by five hundred yards the regiment, without flank scouts or advance scouts. Taught by heavy losses, they modified that a little. But never did they seem to learn the scouting side of cavalry work. Nor did their cavalry seem to know how to follow up a retreat. I have been in several retreats and never were they harassed by the German cavalry.

To give another proof from personal experience: when the Germans, after a victory, were about to enter a town, on three occasions I went forward on a cycle to get in touch with their advance cavalry and make sure of the direction they were taking. Never was there any real ground for uneasiness in doing this, though some press gentlemen once reported me as killed because they saw me cycling out, apparently into the arms of the Uhlans, at Louvain after the battle of Tirlemont. The German cavalry, in short, had no eyes: its courage was of the blind sort and rapidly evaporated on a hot challenge.

Whether the cavalry was able to shine in any charges such as used to be rehearsed so carefully at Potsdam I do not know, not having seen any charges nor encountered an officer who has. Competent observers tell me that both the British and the French artillery have outclassed the German in the heroic combats of Northern France. It is a very high record for them, since the German artillery, from the heaviest to the lightest, is without a doubt extraordinarily good in tactics. The way in which it co-operates with its infantry seems to me specially good. Step by step it follows the infantry advance with patient care, and I have never noticed it either smash up its own men or leave them at a pinch without the moral support of the guns. In return the infantry sticks well to its guns, and I have never noticed, nor have heard recorded, an instance where the German infantry cleared out regardless of the fate of the guns.

In artillery ranging the Germans evidently relied upon:

(1) An excellent system of maps. The area of operations was very minutely set out in numbered squares; and on one battery finding its fire effective on a certain square the number of that square was sent on to as many other batteries as was necessary, and their fire thus could be instantaneously directed on to the required spot. This system of ranging with the aid of squared maps is not peculiar to the German artillery; but it seems to have reached with them a high degree of perfection.

(2) By aeroplanes and captive balloons. The captive balloons usually operated in couples on two flanks; and, I conclude, took cross-observations from two angles of view.

(3) By the use of spies within the lines of their antagonist. This was, probably, their most effective means of ranging. Spies, passing for peasants and wandering about the field of operations, would give signals as to the position of batteries, trenches, and Staff officers.

The absence was noticeable of ranging by "brackets" (i.e., finding a distance by trial firing first at, say, 2,000 and 2,300 yards, then at 2,100, 2,200, and finding the range at 2,050). This system of ranging seems almost obsolete with German batteries.

The moral effect of artillery fire is thoroughly understood and exploited by the Germans. Against infantry in trenches, after finding that shrapnel does not cause a quittance, they try high explosive- less likely to be deadly, but more terrifying. On a wide battlefield a proportion of their guns will fire-seemingly without known aim-at points all over the place. This is evidently not only with the hope of finding a chance mark, but of breeding terror over the whole field, making troops in reserve feel that they, too, are under fire. It is an expensive way of causing fright, but against unseasoned troops can be useful.

The German big guns were laid perfectly. It was always possible to see what they were aimed at and to recognize that the aim was good. In the bombardment of Antwerp in particular I noticed this. The guns clearly had exactly the right elevation and exactly the right deflection. Whether it was intended or not – I think it was-the last stage of that bombardment showed perfection in big gun pointing. Six shells in quick succession came within a few yards of the Hôtel de Ville. I imagined that the idea was to hurry up the burgomaster to come out and surrender. (He had left on that mission at 8.30, just before this bouquet of shells arrived.)

There was no notable horse artillery work on the part of the Germans, so far as I could see or hear.

The artillery worked perfectly "by the book," but without dash or any spirit of adventure. Certainly it was never pushed forward to punish a retreat.

The German infantry has to be credited with a very stubborn courage, but it was, so far as can be judged, chiefly "officers' courage." Left to themselves, the German infantry were prone to surrender: though the same men under their officers would suffer the most severe punishment without flinching.

The virtues and defects alike of the German military system concentrated in the infantry. Educated, partly by godly precept, partly by brutality, into believing that the military officer is a being apart, worthy of worship, the German rank and file follow their officers, or are driven forward by their officers, in positions which seem almost desperate. On the other hand, the German rank and file, deprived of their officers, are more helpless than French or British soldiers in the same circumstances.

In entrenching himself the German soldier is as good as the best (book work and methodical practice!). In taking advantage of natural cover he is inferior to the British (absence of initiative!). The virtues and defects alike of his training send him to the charge in somewhat close order. Thus he is easier to kill but more terrible if he arrives. His marksmanship is inferior to that of the British soldier, but his volley –firing-helped by the flat trajectory of his rifle – can be very effective. He is not fond of the bayonet as a weapon.

Not at all sparing of the infantry when the order to advance is given, the German tactics is nevertheless careful of its infantry in that it practises a very thorough artillery preparation, and, as I have noted before, the artillery follows the infantry step by step.

In regard to minor points, the German air work was far better than was expected in the absence of any special advertisement of her airmen before the war. Her aeroplane proved a very good, very serviceable model, and the aeronauts were, it seemed, standardized. A Taube could always be relied upon for about the same speed and daring. The German commissariat and transport had astonishingly hard work to do, and seemed on the whole to do it very well.

Occasionally the men lacked food; but I do not think they often lacked ammunition. Food problems were in part solved by the system of pillage, but the demands of the wasteful guns had to be supplied from headquarters, and, apparently, always were.

In the villages and towns the individual German soldier showed a tendency to become human and to attempt to fraternize with the inhabitants. Perhaps it was partly because of a fear of the results of this that some of the outrages were organized. Fraternizing with civilians would have deteriorated the discipline, so slavish in its methods, and would have probably led to many desertions.

Summed up, the German Army in the field had all the virtues which a thorough book preparation and a slavish discipline could give. But it was not the ideal army; and, in my judgment, not superior in effectiveness man by man to the French and the British Armies. Comparing it particularly with the British Army, it showed few points of superiority, and several points of inferiority.

A comparison of the various armies (partly the result of my own observation, partly from consultation with officers in the field) led me to this "placing" of the forces:

Staff System.

Germany (with a long lead) 1
France and Great Britain (bracketed) 2
Belgium.. 4

Heavy Artillery.

Germany.. 1
France and Great Britain (bracketed 2
Belgium.. 4

Field Artillery.

France 1
Great Britain 2
Germany and Belgium (bracketed......................... 3

Cavalry.

Great Britain and Belgium (bracketed 1
France 3
Germany.. 4

Infantry.

Great Britain 1
Germany.. 2
France 3
Belgium.. 4

Air Service.

Germany.. 1
Great Britain 2
France 3
Belgium.. 4

In regard to the air service, individual exploits of British airmen were better than those of German airmen, but the whole service of the Germans was better, with its wonderful numbers of standardized fliers and machines.

The idea that the German army followed an absolutely stereo-typed model and could learn nothing from experience is often put forward, but is absurd. Officers and men showed a lack of initiative and were usually inferior in individual intelligence to British, French and Belgians: but the Staff watched every development of the war with keen vigilance and showed a quick faculty of learning. In November a copy fell into my hands of the German Minister for War's letter of advice on the training of the new German armies, dated September 26th. The document gives proof that the German military mind is not impervious to teaching, and that the first stages of the campaign taught it the necessity of some modification of its old tactics.

Summed up, the official instructions insisted on three points: More caution in infantry attack ; the "scrapping" of the cavalry charge; and the further development of aerial reconnaissance, kept in close touch not only with the Commander-in-Chief, but with the artillery command.

The document (translated freely) reads:

Directions for the instruction of new formations of Reserve.

I. It is clear that the putting into the field of new troops is a matter of very great difficulty, but as we have absolute need of these troops by the middle of October to continue the war, it is necessary that these difficulties should be surmounted.

II. In that which concerns the choice of leaders (both officers and non-commissioned officers) it is not so much necessary to respect social grades as to place at each post the man who suits it best.

III. The experience of the war goes to show how expensive it is that the leaders should expose themselves uselessly. It has to be admitted, on the other hand, that men do not hesitate to follow a leader who is actually at their head. But the officer ought not to be in any way distinguishable from his men by his uniform.

Infantry.

IV. It is undoubted that if the German infantry makes good use of entrenching tools, and by this means best utilizes natural cover, so as to shelter itself from the fire of artillery, it is, so to say, unattackable on its front, and, therefore, it has the advantage of the possibility of a strong *échelon* in depth on its flanks.

The greatest possible use of these means (*i.e.*, entrenchment) is recommended to all units, the smallest and the greatest.

None of our adversaries can withstand the German "hourrah!" and the attack with the bayonet.

In the infantry attack it is necessary, above all things, to cross safely the danger zone of the enemy's artillery fire: this may be done by night movements or by movements in foggy weather.

Under such conditions it is generally easy to come into close contact with the infantry of the enemy, particularly when one can pass from an *échelon* in depth to a movement of menace on the flank, however light it may be.

But the end to attain is always to advance up to the artillery of the enemy as quickly as possible and to put it out of action.

Each step in advance ought to be consolidated with the trenching tool against the possibility of a counter offensive.

Cavalry.

V. As regards the cavalry, the habit of pampering horses in peace time has caused some bitter disillusionments for us. It is necessary, therefore, that for the future our horses should be accustomed to bivouac in the open air, and to be satisfied with what food can be obtained on a campaign. Horses should be left out of doors for days together in order to train them to the open-air life.

There is no question at all now of training cavalry horses for dashing work. It is infinitely more important to train them to make long marches at an easy pace from point to point; and to the men it is most important that they should be trained to use their carbines.

The dismounted cavalryman should be able to fight exactly as an infantryman. Cavalry charges no longer play any part in warfare.

Artillery.

VI. The field artillery and the heavy artillery of an army nowadays fight almost exclusively in entrenched positions. Careful attention should be given to the instruction of the artillery in the tactics of entrenchment. The tactics of the search for the enemy's artillery-which is also nearly always in covered positions-are a necessary part of that instruction.

Batteries in this war are often employed from isolated positions in order to take as much advantage as possible of the shelter afforded by the natural features of the country. Nevertheless, fire control to keep the fire of the guns (both as regards rate and direction) at the best possible pitch must be maintained over all the artillery units. Otherwise there would inevitably result an intolerable waste of ammunition.

It is necessary, speaking generally, to attach the highest importance to the economy of ammunition.

Each shot fired uselessly is a crime.

The Air Service.

VII. The role of the aeroplanes in war has taken on an unexpected degree of importance Their work should be carried on in very close connection not only with the general command, but also with the artillery command. Every possible effort should be made on the manoeuvre grounds to train for a close co-operation and a reciprocal understanding between the aeroplane service, the general command, and the artillery.

Aviators on reconnaissances should be provided with pistols and with hand grenades. Though these latter produce no appreciable result for the most part, nevertheless they have an important effect in creating alarm among the enemy, and should therefore be employed.

As regards the "high strategy" of the war, it does not seem to have developed any startling superiority on any side. But there is some evidence that the German generals during the course of the campaign were subjected to what may be called "political" pressure on the part of the Emperor-doubtless with what seemed to him good reasons. It would appear that some time in September, the main immediate objective of the German campaign was changed from the humiliation of France to the invasion of England. That, I think, led to the determined attack on Antwerp and the rush to seize the Channel coast, to be used as the base for air raids and submarine raids against England.

It was curious to note how, just after this, talk of Paris was dropped amongst the Germans, how there was a sudden discovery by them of amiable qualities in the French people, and how there flared up a very fury of objurgation against England. I have from the kindness of an American *attaché* to the Belgian forces, who spoke German perfectly, notes of conversations with a number of German officers (prisoners) which he had just after Turkey came into the conflict on the side of Germany and before the *Emden* was destroyed. The German officers expressed themselves as quite confident of getting through to Dunkirk and Calais, and forming there a base of operations against England. As to the fate of Paris, they professed to be unconcerned, since "the development of the war had made London now the chief objective." Professing respect for France and pity for Belgium, the German officers had an insatiable rage against England.

The entry of Turkey into the conflict they hailed as the beginning of the end for England. Turkey would be able to seize the Suez Canal and shut it against British shipping, and thus paralyse to a large extent British commerce. With the closing of the Suez Canal and the operations of commerce destroyers such as the *Emden* on trade routes still open to Great Britain, and the wearing down of the British naval superiority in minor actions, it would soon be possible to put such economic pressure on England as to fill her land with starving unemployed. The speedy withdrawal of the British Army from the European theatre of war was foreshadowed. "It will have enough to do in defending England and Egypt."

Whilst speaking of the French without contempt and without

extravagant hostility, the German officers expressed confidence in France's ultimate subjection, but "it could wait until after England was dealt with."

To some extent it must have been embarrassing to the German high command to have to change, in a fashion, their objective. The first plan was to capture Paris, force a peace on France, and attack England. The second plan, seemingly, was to let Paris be, but to concentrate on Calais as opening a gate to England, holding the while a defensive grip on the rich districts of Northern France, and using their occupation as a means of bringing economic pressure to force France to turn her thoughts to peace. But to what extent this "political" change of plan was embarrassing to German strategy I cannot pretend to judge. Strategy has not told for much so far in this war. It has been a war of attrition, a mathematical contest. That view of it I put into the mouth of an Irish Sergeant in November.

"It's a murdering war, and all mud and 'rithmetic, which I couldn't bear as man or boy, and no fun at all, at all; but I am not talking against it, because it's a war for the little oppressed nations, and for a most distressful country –

"A country more distressful than old Ireland herself," he added after a pause, on a note of defiance, as if challenging contradiction. Not getting it, he went on a little disappointedly:

"In little Belgium the Prooshians have spared neither the mother nor the babe, the priest nor the holy nun. We have sorrows of our own in Ireland, but it's the Irishman who must take the Belgian to his heart and welcome him among the little distressed nations and show him how an Irishman can fight for a woman who is wronged and whose babe has been murdered.

"Twenty years I have been fighting and drilling all over the world, and sometimes sad about it, too. But what's for an Irishman to do without much book learning except to fight whiles the blood is hot in him?

Now it's glad I am myself to be at this war, fighting for the little peoples, and for the altars.

"But it's a murderous, and it's a mathymatical kind of war:

and if I could I would be ag'in it, having no liking ever, or understanding, of figures, neither algebry, nor Euclid, nor 'rithmetic. As Father O'Flanagan would say, these had no uses for a gentleman provided he had a morsel of Latin to show that there had been education put in him.

"It's all figures, and calculations and motor-cars, this war, and there's little in it of horses, or charges, or aught to amuse an Irishman with the love of fighting for the fun and devilment of it. Give me a battle where the boys feel the spirit in them, and, when the officer gives the word, they go at it for the glory of Heaven, and, though it's five to one, they beat the enemy and chase him to the back of God's-speed. I have been in wars when we fought in a different county, so to speak, every day in the week, from County Dublin to County Meath in a twinkling of a sword.

"But now there's a general in command sitting in an office surrounded by books and a ready-reckoner, and a calculating machine handy. And the engineer-in-chief comes in with the report on the drains: and the general looks serious, and he juggles with a couple of loggy-rithums, and consults the ready-reckoner, and says solemnly: 'We've to get those trenches seven-eighths of an inch deeper, or all is lost.'

"Then the shover-in-chief is called in to the presence, and he reports that one hundred and seventy- one motor-car axles are broken, and that he must have seven hundred and ninety-three new tyres.
But he can't get them, and a regiment or two is ordered out of the battle to patch up a railway embankment somewhere so that that will serve. It's a mighty fine agricultural nation that will come out of this war, with the practice we're having with the spade.

"Then, there's the turn of the higher mathymatics to come. There's a palaver of all the big guns, every man with a pair of compasses and a spirit level, and something on three sticks like a camera, that is used for the making of roads. They begin to throw figures about, and vulgar fractions and cube roots, with a little bit of astronomy thrown in. And the general looks bothered entirely, until a despatch comes in from the boss doctor, and his face lights up as he reads it.

"'Bhoys,' he says, gay-like, 'our scouts report that in trench Number one thousand one hundred and thirty-seven of the enemy there are one hundred and forty-nine cases of collywobbles. We shall attack to-night.' And carried away by the glory of the moment he is startled out of his impassive calm and rapidly turning over the pages of his algebra book and making calculations, he cries: 'If the boys of England, not forgetting Ireland and Scotland, do their duty, we shall win back one yard three inches of territory or twenty-three-decimal-seven-seven-nine of us die in the attempt.'

"Oh, he's a powerful man with figures, is the general; and it's right he is ordinarily. But it's a dull thing is war, with all this mathymatics and mud and sitting down while the figures are worked out; and with even the guns fired by a table of decimals. To an Irishman it would be intolerable entirely if it were not for the thought of the poor little Belges and their distresses."

Sergeant Clancy was silent for a moment. We waited, hoping he would go on. In a moment he did. "Perhaps another way will be found out of it all, after all; somebody one day will have forgotten his book of figures, and he'll find a way of going at it in the old way, just getting into the thick of it, and fighting until the enemy finds he is wanted somewhere else and chasing him from the Liffey to the Shannon. He will be a general with Irish blood in him, if he comes, I am after thinking."

Tolstoi, before his death, predicting the great European war, said that out of it would arise a general of original genius. If his prophecy comes true, let us pray that the genius does not develop on the German side! The German Army is proving (and will prove) quite a tough enough one to subdue, even with generalship which is not inspired by genius, and which seems to be subject to some interference with its very high degree of talent by the Emperor. If there had been a Napoleon at its head that magnificent machine, the German Army, would by today have held the continent of Europe from the Atlantic to the Viatula.

CHAPTER XI

OSTEND: THE HEROIC KING

BEFORE following the retreat of the Belgian Army from Antwerp to its last seat at ———— * it will be of interest to turn a backward glance at Brussels, and note how it fared under German rule. To the credit of the Germans let it be said that there were no atrocities there to the date of writing (January, 1915). Whilst I was at Antwerp a Belgian journalist friend went in and out of Brussels for me and kept me acquainted with events there.

The day following the occupation the invaders seized all the Ministries, of War, Foreign Affairs, Agriculture, and Public Works. They also occupied the Chamber of Deputies and the Senate buildings, and the railway stations. After they had been in possession a few days they took the Palais de Justice and the King's Palace at Laeken.

The citizens remained frigid and calm, watching the invasion of the "rats," as they call them (the German uniforms strongly suggest the grey rat), with resignation and with confidence in the ultimate issue of the conflict. Many continued to wear in their buttonholes a *cocarde* or ribbon of the national colours. The German permitted this. But of French and English national decorations he was not so tolerant, often going to the length of snatching the *cocarde* or the ribbon from off the breast of the wearer. The Belgian flag was still left floating in many places in the town, among others on the Hôtel de Ville, and on each of the towers of the Church of Ste. Gudule. The communal authorities of Brussels, with the assistance of certain ministerial officials, acting by arrangement with the German military government, took from the outset all the measures necessary for the provisioning of the town. The necessities of life were kept at a moderate price.

---

*The name of the town which is the temporary seat of the Belgian Army it is perhaps still necessary to suppress. Probably the Germans know quite well all about it; but it will do no harm to be careful.

The German Governor in the middle of September posted a proclamation forbidding the showing of Belgian flags from the houses. The proclamation, conspicuously moderate in tone, disavowed any intention to wound the sentiment and dignity of the inhabitants, but stated that the display of Belgian flags might provoke conflicts. Burgomaster Max followed this with a proclamation, in which he acknowledged the courteous terms of the German order, but added that it would no less wound the profoundly ardent and proud population of Brussels. He begged the citizens to accept provisionally the fate imposed upon them and withdraw the flags, waiting patiently for the hour of reparation.

This proclamation led to the arrest of M. Max, and he was brought before General von Luttwitz, Military Governor of Brussels, who rated the Burgomaster for having published a placard without having received th2e previous authorization of the German Government, a publication which constituted a grave act of disobedience to the German authorities and a plain defiance of them. And he spread out before M. Max's eyes the text of his proclamation, whereon the following phrases had been underlined:

"The proclamation will, none the less, profoundly wound the ardent and proud population of Brussels. Let us provisionally accept the fate imposed upon us.
. . . Let us patiently await the hour of reparation."

General von Luttwitz proceeded to inform him that he was to be placed under arrest. To this M. Max only replied: "Very well."
General von Luttwitz proceeded: "We are going to send you to Germany; we are going to send you to Berlin."
M. Max again replied: "Very well."
Nonplussed by M. Max's calm and resolute demeanour, General von Luttwitz left him and went to make a report to Marshal von der Goltz, Military Governor of Belgium. The conference lasted a quarter of an hour, at the end of which time General von Luttwitz came back to the Burgomaster and said: "We think there is probably a way of arranging matters."

"How so?" asked M. Max.

"Look here," was the reply; "you will proceed to cover with blank sheets of paper the placards you have had put up."

"I understand," said M. Max; "but I will only do it on condition that you give me formal instructions to that effect in writing. But perhaps it would be better that you should yourself cover up my placards. You have men specially appointed to deal with public notices."

"Very well, then, we will see to it," said General von Luttwitz.

M. Max, by his coolness and courage, "scored" often in his reign as Burgomaster at Brussels during the German occupation. On one occasion the German authorities forbade the people to keep carrier pigeons. Now, the Brussels people are great pigeon fanciers, and pigeon races are one of the favourite sports of the working classes. Naturally the people were furious, and many owners of pigeons refused to destroy them. M. Max intervened, and at his suggestion the Germans agreed that the pigeons should be collected together at a certain place and there placed under the surveillance of German soldiers. The place chosen was one of the great halls of the Parc du Cinquantenaire, and here hundreds of baskets full of pigeons were deposited, the owners coming every day to feed these strange prisoners of war.

Such incidents put M. Max in a very good light, and reflect credit, too, on the Germans, who in Brussels proved that they could behave decently in some respects.

Later, the German authority fell out with M. Max on the question of money. Soon after the occupation the Germans talked of making the city and the Province of Brabant pay a war levy of 500,000,000 francs. M. Max would not listen to the mention of such a sum, and simply refused to discuss it. After seven days spent in negotiations the Germans reduced their claim and fixed at 50,000,000 francs the sum payable by the city of Brussels. They informed M. Max of this decision, and announced to him that the money must be paid within a short space of time. M. Max did not agree to the figure named by the German Military Governor, but he undertook to pay twenty million francs in five weeks, four millions a week. The Germans agreed to accept this arrangement, and week by week regularly received the four millions. The payment of the last instalment fell due about the end of September. On Friday, the 25th of the month, M. Max was summoned to appear before General von der Goltz, who inquired if the money would be forthcoming. The Burgomaster replied that he had the sum in question at disposal, and that he proposed to hand it over in a day or two. Thereupon the General reminded M. Max that the war contribution leviable was not twenty million francs, but fifty, and that it would therefore be necessary, when the twenty millions had been paid, to find another thirty millions. "Impossible!" exclaimed M. Max, "quite impossible! I won't undertake to find the money. I have no means of procuring anything like it; moreover, I made myself responsible for no more than twenty millions."

This gave rise to a stormy discussion between the Burgomaster and the German authorities, who finally threatened to adopt serious measures. These latter turned out to be the placarding of the walls of Brussels (during the night of September 25-26) with notices informing the inhabitants that, as the payment of the war levy had not been completed, the obligations incurred by the Germans would no longer be discharged, but would for the future be deferred till the end of the war.

On hearing this, M. Max (on the ground that the Germans had failed to carry out the arrangement previously made) decided to withhold payment of the final four million francs, which he deposited in a place of safety The result of this was that he was arrested and sent to Germany. His arrest was a serious blow to the citizens of Brussels, but it was not followed-as some anticipated-by any outburst of atrocity on the part of the German conquerors in Brussels. I have seen a Brussels citizen who left the place as recently as November 3rd last, and he told me (November 14th) that the citizens missed M. Max and keep him in affectionate remembrance, but in his absence the civil government of the city proceeds smoothly enough, as the Germans continue to be on their good behaviour. The citizens cherish the hope that their immunity from outrages will continue, as there has been a notable amelioration of German conduct in other parts of Belgium since it began to be clear to the German Emperor that henceforth the campaign is a defensive one for his people and that the tide of invasion will soon turn.

There is no famine in Brussels. Necessarily there is a great deal of distress among the poor, for there is much unemployment, but food supplies, with the exception of bread, are not scarce. Bread is dearer, fruit and vegetables much cheaper than usual. Meat is at a normal price. For the ordinary *ménage* the cost of living is, if anything, less than before the war. The population of Brussels is at least as great as before the war.

Many prisoners have passed through Brussels on their way to Germany. They are paraded as much as possible before the inhabitants. The citizens do their best to help the prisoners with food and comforts as the trains pass through. They notice that the British prisoners are looked upon with special malignity by the Germans and have harsher treatment than other prisoners.

*   *   *   *   *

To take up again the history of the Belgian Army in retreat from Antwerp. After the fall of that city I went to London for two days and subsequently rejoined the Belgian Army at—— ——. Particulars of the actions south-west of Antwerp, between the dates October 7th and October 14th, when the Belgian Army and the British Marines retreated from the fortified area towards the coast, were communicated to me by combatant officers. On October 7th the withdrawal of the Belgian cavalry and the armoured mitrailleuse cars was effected. They were no longer of any great use on the field of operations around Antwerp, and there was already a reasonable certainty that they would be needed to guard, as far as possible, the line of retreat. The chief danger of the position was that the Germans would cross the river at Termonde in force, and thus cut off the line of retreat towards the coast, forcing the whole Belgian Army and the British contingent towards the Dutch frontier. From Great Britain a force was sent to help to cover the retreat, but its gallant operations do not come within the limits of my story. In the covering of the retreat very good work was done by the Belgian cavalry and mitrailleuse cars, with some help from the artillery and the carabineer cyclists; and they can claim a good share of the credit for having held back the Germans for a sufficient time to enable the forces evacuating Antwerp to pass to the coast. Of course the retreating army had to do its share of the fighting, but the advance guard had saved them from finding the enemy actually established on the road. The German cavalry (chiefly Bavarian) was very heavily punished by the Belgian cavalry and by the Belgian armoured cars.

The German force operating south-west from Antwerp was estimated at about forty thousand. That number passed through Ghent and then split up into two forces, one body of about thirty thousand going towards Courtrai, the other of about ten thousand towards the coast. The German force was well supplied with artillery, especially with howitzers of large calibre.

It was not possible in all the circumstances to do more than delay and harass the German advance, as some of the troops in retreat had had such a fatiguing experience as to be quite incapable of further fighting for a time. All accounts agree that the force, hard as it had been punished and severe as were the trials of the retreat, showed no loss of morale. Officers stuck to their posts and their men to them.

Though some lacked experience, none lacked courage. Some incidents of personal gallantry and skill lighten up the chapter of retreat. The six Belgian armoured mitrailleuse cars did splendid service from Wednesday, October 7th, to Tuesday, October 13th, and to their efforts during the six days is attributed a loss of the enemy's cavalry to the extent of eight hundred. In particular one car surprised a squadron of the enemy's cavalry dismounted, killed several at 250 yards' range, stampeded all the horses, and captured the field wireless telegraph wagon of No. 2 Light Wireless Corps of the Third Bavarian Division, including all its records.

Another incident of the retreat. A Belgian cavalry officer, who has a good record during this war, had to leave in the course of retreat his father's chateau. He had collected there a great number of captured trophies of the war, such as Uhlans' helmets and lances, and these shared a room with a great number of trophies he had won in international sporting competitions. One of these sports trophies was a silver cup won at Frankfort, Germany. He left this, surrounded by Uhlans' helmets, and a card stating that he had won it "by mistake in competing with Germans" and begging that it should be sent back to Germany.

By Thursday, October 15th, the last of the Belgian troops had evacuated Ostend. The last man out, practically, was the Belgian General, and his retirement was covered only by armoured motor-cars.

Nothing was left in Ostend for the Germans but two trainloads of provisions. These were left because, through a misunderstanding, a railway bridge was blown up a little too soon. Some German patrols were actually in the suburbs of Ostend on the previous evening (Wednesday), but no German force entered until Thursday, when about two hundred arrived by tram. (In this very mechanical war the tram and the motor-bus come into the sphere of action as well as the railway train.)

On the retreat King Albert and his Queen showed a noble courage. I am told by those who were around him during these sad days that he resisted firmly, even indignantly, all the suggestions which were made to him to retire into France and safety. For her part the Queen insisted that her place was by his side. Forced out of Antwerp, the royal couple retired but a day's march towards the coast. When their place of retreat (St. Nicholas) came under the German guns they retired to Selzaete, both King and Queen encouraging the troops in their gallant rear-guard actions. Ostend was the next stage in this pilgrimage. It was with the greatest difficulty that the King could be induced to leave that city, the last great populous centre of his kingdom, and again he refused to cross the border into France, though the Belgian Government retired to Havre. The value of his example to his army cannot be exaggerated. I believe that all Belgium would have passed over to the invader during those October days if the King had taken the prudent course and gone to France.

Writing later (November 8th), I commented:

"The heroic figure in this war is King Albert of the Belgians, whose devotion to duty and personal courage rallied the Belgian Army within the last few miles left of their country, and inspired them to turn and push back the invader. His resolution during the painful retreat from Antwerp, his determination to resist the advice given to him to take refuge in France, have had perhaps more than any other single influence the greatest efficacy in making the Belgian Army what it is today-a band of soldiers worthy of comparison with the Old Guard. The Belgian Army can be seen reacting to his influence. One recent day the Germans engaged in a spiteful bombardment of Fumes. The King had business that day in the town with his Staff. He did not permit the bombardment to disturb him. Word of this passed through the ranks. The next day two Belgian regiments, with two French regiments, by a bayonet charge that could not be denied, won the key to the battle of the Yser; and the Belgians had been continuously in the trenches for sixteen days.

" 'We like to do something for the King,' said one soldier simply, when he was congratulated on his share in the battle, he having kept on with the bayonet to the end, in spite of a flesh wound from a rifle-ball.

"The King of the Belgians is the real, active, directing Commander-in-Chief of his Army. His Staff offices are quite near to the front, and he is at his 'office' early in the morning, sometimes as early as eight o'clock, rarely later than nine. At midday a little inn near by sends to him luncheon.

It is very simple; sometimes it is lacking even in what a middle-class citizen of London would regard as the ordinary comforts of the table. The King could get anything that he wanted if he chose to employ the military transport to bring it up from a port on the coast. He is so vitally absorbed in his work, however, as to be indifferent to his own comfort. So long as he can get a cigar after luncheon he is satisfied, and even that has been sometimes lacking. "In the afternoon the King's labours continue. He has visits to receive and to make. He constantly visits the trenches. Of late he has wisely decided that the Belgian Army would be encouraged in its task if it saw a little of the ceremony and panoply of war. So reviews are fairly frequent. When there is a chance for a regiment, passing from one part of the front to the other, to march past the King with music at its head, the chance is taken.

"Sometimes it is nine in the evening before the King leaves his Staff office, but more usually six or seven. Going to his temporary palace-which German airmen are always seeking out with their bombs, but which happily they have not yet found-he continues then to carry on the work of State. But his day's labour in the public eye stretches to an average of eight or nine hours. It is carried on in a council-chamber well fitted for this King who has restored to memory the primitive virtues of kings. In one of those fine Middle Age buildings which every Belgian town has, is a chamber panelled in old oak and hung round with gilt-stamped leather; the table and chairs are of the Middle Ages, so, too, is the great open fireplace. Here a King worthy to have sat at the Round Table does his work in a fit setting."

On October 15th, after leaving Ostend, the Belgian Army, inspired by good leadership, rallied, turned back, actually won Ostend again for a few hours, and then taking up a stand on the River Yser, a little south, prepared to do a service to the cause of the Allies which equalled that of Liége.

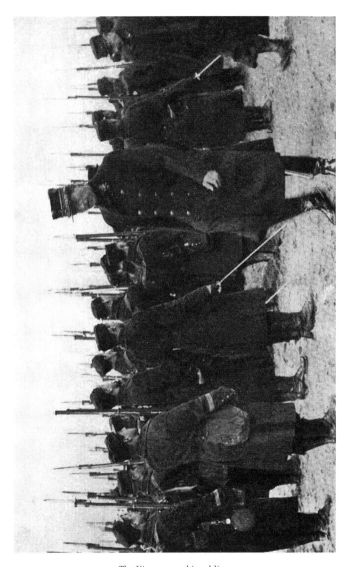

The King among his soldiers

CHAPTER XII

THE BATTLE OF THE YSER

IT was with the Battle of the Yser that the Belgian Army came first into actual line with their allies; and the encouragement of feeling a friendly hand near showed itself in their work. I doubt if all through the war there has been a better achievement than the holding of the line of the Yser by the Belgian Army during October.

Taking the operations of the main forces of the Allies into consideration, they divide themselves naturally under the headings of the Battle of the Marne, the Battle of the Aisne, and the Battle of Flanders. But this last battle has two such distinct phases that it can be most conveniently considered under headings clearly marked-the operations on the Yser and the operations around Ypres. These together checked the effort of the Germans to turn the left wing of the Allies and destroyed for a time their hope of seizing Dunkirk and Calais and attacking the sea communication between France and Great Britain. The operations around Ypres did not take on their full importance until the Germans had definitely failed in their effort to pierce the line of the Allies between the sea and Dixmude (that is to say, the line of the Yser), and thus to reach Dunkirk by the shortest route. The Battle of Flanders had then for its first phase the Battle of the Yser, for its second the Battle of Ypres, with the first phase sharply distinct from the second.

After Liége, when was broken the force of the first violent blow of the Germans aimed against good faith in keeping treaties, the Belgian Army had not a day's rest from fighting. Feeble in numbers, attacked just as it was in the middle of reorganization, it struggled, nevertheless, courageously against the mass of the invaders, but always using up its numbers pitifully during the violent combats, which had to be followed by retreats imposed upon it by the superior numbers and armaments of the adversary. When it was threatened with being surrounded in Antwerp and made captive, it retired from that position, executing a retreat which by its rapidity inflicted a bitter disappointment on the Germans. But this retreat, particularly fatiguing and demoralizing, depressed the spirits of the Army and imposed logically the necessity of a period of repose for reorganization.

Unhappily, the development of the campaign deprived it of the chance of the repose which was so sternly necessary. New German forces came into the attack with the plan of prolonging the German line towards the sea and of enveloping the left wing of the Franco-British Army. Further, the German Army which had carried on the siege of Antwerp, freed from that task, advanced rapidly upon the Belgian Army in retreat.

The situation for the Allied forces had its grave possibilities of embarrassment. The road to Dunkirk and Calais would be open to the Germans if some army had not opposed immediately an obstacle to the advance of the German Army. Instead of taking a period of rest for reorganization, the Belgian Army came to a halt on the line of the Yser and awaited the attack. It was aided at Dixmude by a brigade of French Marines, but the Belgian line held the line of the Yser from Dixmude to the sea.

It set out on that line its six divisions.

My diary of October 16th records:

"I recognize the necessity of discounting in my own mind the favourable impressions formed, of making a very great allowance for the affection one must feel for these plucky Belgians after nearly three months of close companionship with them. It would be unnatural if one did not at first see the rosy side of things and have an inclination to hope for the best. But making all allowance for that and seeking to get to a critical non-sympathetic view, I can frankly say that I have been astonished to find things as good as they are. The Belgian Army after its plucky campaign at Liége and its equally plucky and clever field campaign around Tirlemont was overwhelmed in the flood of the German invasion about the middle of last August. Since then it has always had to face great odds, and has had its morale constantly attacked by the German policy of taking requital for a Belgian victory in the field by burning a town and massacreing a civil population. Now that Antwerp, the last citadel of the Belgian nation, has fallen temporarily into the hands of the enemy, it would be pardonable if the Belgian Army, almost forced off its own soil, were to decide that the time had come to throw down arms and seek quiet.

"But none of that spirit shows. The men have come out of their troubles with courage undaunted, and are coming eagerly to the new rallying point. I see many slightly wounded men coming back to the colours. In some cases, of course, there are soldiers but not companies or regiments to be reckoned with. But to an astonishing degree, in view of all the circumstances, the organization of the army is intact. I noted one infantry regiment in particular, marching through the streets with a regular swagger. It was a little circumstance-that swagger, pretty as it looks, is not necessary for the winning of battles, as the French show with their less impressive but terribly effective marching-but it had its significance as showing the spirit of the men who intend to fight on, and intend also, clearly enough, to pick up any new points they can about the method of fighting.

"Our little brother who stood out so valiantly during those early days of August, saving precious hours, finds himself now getting full credit for his pluck. He is not expected to be downcast at his trials, but to be proud of his achievements."

The event fully justified this optimism on my part.

On October 15th the line of the Yser was occupied, and the battle began on the next day by a German attack upon Dixmude, but this was not more than a reconnaissance in force to search out a way across the Yser. The attack was bravely repulsed by the French Marines with the help of the Belgian field Artillery; the brigade of French Marines did not have any artillery of their own at the time, and therefore Belgian artillery had been attached to them.

On October 17th the first German shells searched the advance posts held by the Belgian Army. On October 18th a violent and stubborn attack was opened. It was continued without any abatement of violence up to October 30th.

The struggle for the possession of the advance posts was stern. In the afternoon of October 18th the advance posts of

Mannekensvere and Keyem were lost, in spite of the stubborn resistance of the Belgian troops, because of the sheer weight of German numbers. But that night, by an energetic counter-attack, we won back Keyem from the Germans. On October 19th the German attack was redoubled in intensity. The enemy had been forced to recognize the strength of the Belgian resistance, and now tried to overcome it by a more energetic effort. The advance post of Lombartzyde repulsed three successive assaults. Beerst was, however, lost. Keyem continued to resist. Finally, to draw away attention from our centre, on which the most violent German attacks seemed to be concentrated, the commander of the Belgian Army ordered a counter-attack from the direction of Dixmude by the French Marines and a Belgian division. This counter-attack was launched on the German front between Beerst and Vladsloo. At the fall of night the southern environs of Beerst and the village of Vladsloo were in the possession of the Allies. On this part of their front the Germans had been taken in the flank.

But at this moment we heard of the arrival from the direction of Roulers of a considerable new force of the enemy. Our troops which had sallied out of Dixmude would have run great danger of being cut off if they had pursued their movement of advance. So the necessity was imposed upon our command to recall them behind the defensive line of the Yser. That night Keyem was reoccupied by the Germans.

On the 20th the enemy continued his offensive. Artillery of all calibre drenched our trenches with shells, and repeated attempts were made to pierce our line. In front of Nieuport the Germans captured the Farm of Bambuig, but this success was at first but momentary. They had scarcely taken possession of the place when a counter-attack turned them out again. They returned, however, to the charge, and succeeded finally that evening in obtaining and keeping possession of this important advance post.

At the same time towards Dixmude there was a violent German attack, in which a great force was employed. But the French Marines, reinforced by a Belgian brigade, repulsed the attack and inflicted very heavy losses on the enemy. The Germans renewed the attack that night, but with no more success. On other parts of the battle front during the night a bombardment of almost unexampled violence was kept up.

On October 21st, in the early morning, another German attack was launched upon Dixmude, and again the German force was driven back with heavy losses. But time was short for the Germans. They recognized that at all costs it was necessary to pierce our defensive line before our reinforcements (which had been called up as the seriousness of the German attack became clear) could arrive. In the afternoon simultaneous German assaults were launched upon Schoorbakke and Dixmude.

They both were checked; but the check was only to the fierce, untiring attacks of the infantry; there was no check to the furious cannonading, the effects of which were truly terrifying. At the fall of night the German attack was resumed upon Dixmude and the trenches bordering the Yperlee Canal (running south from Dixmude). This attack only served to add to the height of the heaps of German dead before the trenches of the defenders.

This violent struggle-sustainer by the Belgian Army at a time when it was already worn out with many battles, and when it was hoping for a little rest behind the lines of the Allies after experiencing much fatigue-could it go on? The losses of the Belgian force were considerable; its companies were decimated, the disorganization of its units through losses was great. It had held out for five days, with the sole help of a brigade of French Marines and of the British squadron which from the sea crushed such of the Germans as came within range of its guns. How much longer now could the Belgian Army hold out without reinforcements?

In the forenoon of the 22nd the ships of the British squadron resumed their bombardment of the German position. As on previous days, no reply came from the German batteries. What the effect of this naval bombardment was there was no means of knowing, except from the accounts of German prisoners and the somewhat scanty observation on our side. But it seems to have been very good; and there was reason to entertain the belief that it had been efficacious in keeping the Germans from establishing heavy artillery with which to bombard Furnes- not a fortified place nor of any military importance, but the largest town near the fighting area, and a natural mark, therefore, for

German guns. On Wednesday, the 21st, the German heavy guns had found the range of the town, and dropped five shells just short of the railway station. No more shells came then. The bombardment of the town, which seemed immediately inevitable, was mysteriously postponed. Why? The most natural conclusion was that the German heavy batteries were put out of action, temporarily at least, by our artillery. A naval 12-inch shell loaded with lyddite would do all that was wanted for a heavy land battery if it fell in the right place.

Besides their value in acting as heavy batteries on our left flank the British warships were cheerful to think that they were acting as "ground-bait " for the German Fleet. There is much evidence from German prisoners of the intense irritation felt in the German lines at this participation of the British Fleet in a land action. It was thought possible for a time that this irritation would lead to a serious attempt on the part of German naval forces to take a hand in the conflict.

During the forenoon of October 22nd, particularly on our left flank: (the sea flank) dominated by the British batteries, there was a period almost of calm, the German attack dwindling away. This was interpreted as a sign that they intended to add to their artillery strength. But apparently this was not so, for in the afternoon without more than the usual artillery preparation the German infantry attempted the passage of the river at a point between Nieuport and Dixmude, nearer to the former than the latter town. The Belgian force tried a ruse of war and allowed a bridge to be thrown across the river at a point thoroughly commanded by their guns. The Germans advanced with confidence, reckoning that our artillery had been silenced.

As soon as a regiment had crossed our guns opened fire, destroyed the bridge and then turned their fire on the German force which had crossed. The infantry followed this up with an effective fire at close range and, finally, with a bayonet charge. The Germans were thrown back across the river with very severe loss, many being drowned in addition to those killed by rifle-fire and the bayonet.

It was interesting to note on the battlefield this day that the Belgian infantry had learned contempt for the big high-explosive shell which the Germans use in field operations, as a means of terrorism rather than of destruction. At Dixmude whilst the big shells were making fireworks, a Belgian soldier of the line, going about his duties without flurry, addressed a big shell as it passed screaming through the air:

"Ah, my boy. You are finished. We know all about you now!"

In truth, in the field the big high-explosive shell rarely pays for its powder. It is efficacious only against forts, and for killing civilians in houses.

The defence of the Belgians during the 22nd was splendid. But these brave soldiers were now at the end of their strength. A new night attack delivered during a violent storm of wind and rain by freshly-arrived German troops overcame them. Tervaete was that night in the hands of the Germans.

Happily, friendly reinforcements were announced, and the news galvanized Belgian energies to fresh activity. The struggle was continued bravely along all the front during October 23rd, the Belgians holding back the Germans on the left bank of the Yser whilst a French division replaced a part of the Belgian Army on the left wing between Nieuport and the sea. That night the Germans launched a new attack against Dixmude. It was repulsed by the French Marines and two Belgian regiments. From October 24th, the struggle went on with no less intensity, but now the Belgian Army had the extra help of a French division and of some battalions of French territorials. It was enough to inspire them with fresh courage. The ground won by the Germans within the head of the Yser between Schoorbakke and Tervaete was violently bombarded by the artillery of the Allies. A whole German division had established itself there. Our artillery punished it savagely. Later there was found on the body of an officer of the German 22nd Corps of Reserve a field note-book, in which he told the terrible story of these days of "frightful combats," in "the hell" which the artillery fire of the Allies created, a hell from which he could not get out.

"The enormous losses," this German officer noted, "have disorganized all our 44th Division; the companies are reduced to half their strength; most of the officers have been killed; the units are so mixed up that it is impossible to tell one from another. The men cannot eat, nor drink, nor sleep any more, and die desperate, feeling that all their losses are in vain."

But the German attack continued; the ground on the left bank of the Yser, between the river and the railway line, Nieuport-Dixmude, was won by them foot by foot.

The German force was so much greater in numbers that it could not be withstood successfully. Still every inch of the way was contested, and meanwhile a new defensive line was prepared, based on the railway line behind the river. To recount day by day the incidents of the Battle of the Yser would be tedious. In spite of the fierce and sometimes the heroic character of the fighting the story would repeat itself day by day. After fourteen days there were the same things to be said as after four days.

Furious bombardments began and ended seemingly when the supply of ammunition ran short, and then began again. There were attacks and counter-attacks by the infantry; then periods when the men went to sleep standing up in their trenches and mutual exhaustion put a limit to the slaughter for a term. Then fresh troops arrived (or troops who after seven days in the trenches had had one day of peace in the rear and were fresh enough to make a new effort), and the killing began again.

On October 28th, I summed up the position as it was then:

"The Battle of the Yser continues with a stubbornness which, according to those in a position to judge, gives it the first place in this war of long siege battles. For twelve days now the same men have held the trenches on our side, and during all that time there was only one period of twelve hours of what might be called desultory fighting, and that was yesterday afternoon and evening when, the Germans having won a definite passage across the Yser, were too fatigued to follow up the advantage, and the two armies glared at one another, inert, each alike helpless to wound further for the moment. The Belgians have opened the dykes around Dixmude, and flood waters invade now the German trenches.

"This morning the fighting was renewed with fierce energy. Villages which had been bombarded and in part burned found their ruins searched again by continuous shrapnel and high-explosive shell-fire.

Trenches in which wearied men had learned to sleep under

heavy fire became feverishly awake under a fusillade more intense than any they had known before. And the German infantry (reinforced) began to push forward, gaining a little terrain here and there, then again losing it, and then gaining it again.

"Behind their effort could be seen the firmest resolve to win through on this coast line at any cost. How many men the enemy have engaged on this section of the front it is difficult to estimate with certainty. But calculations go as high as 150,000. Truly, whether it reaches that figure or not it is a great force, and in so far as the high command and the artillery arm are concerned, it is a first-class force. The same cannot be said of the infantry, which, judging by the prisoners taken, is largely made up of youths and poorly-trained men. Allowing that it is the worst element of the force which finds its way to the rear of its antagonists' lines without its arms, still the German Army in front of Nieuport-Dixmude must be considered as made up in large part of inferior infantry. Nevertheless, with their great superiority in numbers and their re-established artillery superiority, they shape as if they were equal to the task of winning some further ground yet before the moment of repulse comes.

"A stirring spectacle was that of the British warship *Venerable,* acting as a heavy battery on our left flank this morning. Steaming slowly up and down the coast between La Panne and Coxyde, the *Venerable* fired broadside after broadside into the German batteries from her twelve-inch guns.

Sometimes four of these guns were discharged at once. From the muzzles came a thin puff of smoke, enveloping a great ball of fire, which seemed to rush from the muzzle a yard or two and then move back towards it a little before vanishing. The huge shells with their charge of lyddite could be seen smashing in the German lines, the fall of each marked by a pall of green-black smoke.

"The German infantry, despite this fire depriving them of artillery support, kept up their right flank position on the seacoast, whilst their main forward attack was developed by the villages Ramscappelle, Boutshouche, and Pervyse. Around Dixmude the low-lying areas had been inundated with water drawn from the Yser and the canal near by; and this waterlogged area acted (just as the British naval guns acted on the sea line) as an aid to the Allies' defensive position. Practically the German movement of attack was thus limited to a line which can be found most easily by dividing the line from Nieuport to Dixmude into three equal parts and taking the central one.

"In the afternoon German big guns which had been brought into positions came into action against the town of Furnes. Only two shells were fired. Both did no damage. But a panic seized the town of Furnes. All kinds of reassuring and comforting stories were spread about: the most 'reassuring' that the shells were strays from the British warship; another that a Taube had dropped two bombs. But clearly the enemy had now guns forward, and a bombardment was possible with the evening.

"The panic in the town quietened in about an hour as no more shells fell. But many left the town. The battle meanwhile continued. For the soldiers in the fields these big shells have no terrors. In the trenches the Belgian soldiers after twelve days of continuous fighting keep their positions and their courage. They even find time in the trenches between outbursts of firing to fashion rude effigies in clay of the German soldiers, and these are represented sometimes with a little bread in their mouths – a cruel mirth; but who can blame it? Our troops so far have been fed well in the trenches, and have not had hunger added to their trials. The German commissariat seems to have failed. The German prisoners come in gaunt, pallid, mere ghosts of men. In the case of one batch of thirty-five they were captured through one of their number rushing forward, arms in the air, and offering himself as prisoner; on being taken he led his captors up to his mates, who joyfully surrendered.

"Nevertheless, the majority of the Germans hold their trenches and advance from them when ordered-tribute to the iron discipline which can thus keep rule over war-weary, starved men.

"The German troops on the Belgian front (i.e., the Yser front and the Ypres front) now are in numbers and dispositions somewhat like this: On the coast dunes there are four divisions of the Ersatz Reserve, next to them (coming along the line south-east) are ranged the 2nd Army Corps, the 22nd Army Corps, the 23rd Army Corps, the 26th Army Corps (at Roulers), some Ersatz and Landwehr troops in reserve, four divisions of cavalry, the 19th Army Corps, and around Lille, the 18th, 13th and 14th Army Corps, with a great force of cavalry. If these observations are correct there are about 600,000 German troops between Ostend and Lille."

The expected bombardment of Furnes came later in the week, but did no great harm. Some thirty shells were fired into the town, of which only ten exploded. The only notable casualty was that a nun praying in her convent had her leg broken by a fragment of shell. One shell pierced the roof of the Noble Rose Hotel, whilst a number of officers were there at lunch. Lunch proceeded after a minute's interruption.

The inundation had given the Germans a new enemy to fight, an enemy against which they could do nothing. For them to conquer now one means only was available: to rush forward, to pierce the line of the defence behind which would be found firm foothold. To retreat would be to confess defeat. The battle of the Yser came now to its fiercest and most bloody point. The Germans attacked with the desperation of the last effort. On October 30th their attack carried the village of Ramscappelle, *point d'appui* of the whole line. The position then was critical for the Allies, but soon some battalions of the French division and two Belgian divisions threw themselves forward to retake the village.

The firm establishment of the Germans there on the main road from Ostend to Dunkirk might have ultimately made necessary the falling back of our whole line. During the night of Friday, October 30th, therefore, our attack was planned. The German trenches were kept uneasy throughout the night with constant artillery fire and several feint attacks. But the real attack was not launched until the dawn. Then the German trenches were showered with shrapnel and with high-explosive shell from the big batteries, whilst the watching infantry tool: every opportunity for a volley.

At six our infantry (two regiments of Belgians and an equal force of French) came out of their trenches and, with a rush and a cheer, crossed the ground between them and the enemy and were into their trenches with the bayonet. The Germans fought well and with coolness. They had literally to be cut out of the trenches. Man grappled with man in the blood-flowing ditches, and the loss in killed and wounded was desperate. But our infantry was the stronger when it came to this hand-to-hand fighting, and the Germans were forced to run. As they turned, fire was opened on them, and then they rallied and seemed to try to hold the railway embankment, thinking perhaps that our force had occupied their trenches and opened fire from them. But the Belgian-French infantry had been firing as they advanced, and, now coming on, finished their task completely with the bayonet, pushing right on to the railway embankment.

The field after the battle, at nine o'clock in the morning, was a sight of horror. Not a yard but had something of the dreadful *débris* of slaughter. Probably at least five thousand were killed and wounded altogether, and the killed were in far greater proportion than the wounded. Of the two Belgian regiments engaged in the combat, one crowned with its share in this achievement sixteen days' continuous fighting in the trenches. It had held a point of the Yser against the German bridge makers for four days and nights of that period almost without an hour's rest.

In their advance to re-establish their forward posts in those parts of the *terrain* which emerged from out of the flood, the Belgians found on the roads the German slain in heaps (and among them many wounded, whom the Germans had not had time to take away); some engulfed cannon; arms and *matériel* in great quantities-in fact, all the signs of a precipitate retreat.

Friends in Arms – The two Kings in happier times

CHAPTER XIII

THE TIDE TURNS

OCTOBER closed gloriously for the Belgian Army. After a week, in which sometimes doubt and fear had predominated, and during which there were actual preparations once to evacuate the last scrap of Belgium, a fine victory had been won and a general advance seemed in sight. But November was not altogether a cheerful month. For one thing, a survey of the late battlefield did not suggest cheerfulness. The battle front Nieuport-Dixmude had been ravaged to a greater extent, perhaps, than any other area in this war. The cannon engaged on each side numbered at least five hundred. Included in them were British naval guns firing lyddite shell and German naval guns and 28-centimetre howitzers. For three full weeks they were engaged in battering at the buildings and tearing at the entrenchments. The final result recalled San Francisco after the earthquake and fire.

Indeed the destruction was generally more complete, the suggestion of powers of destruction unloosed more terrible. Along the line of the Yser for eight or ten miles, man had seemed to act with the deliberate intention of destroying all trace of civilization. The roads had been torn up in every direction by great shells. Craters-the pits which the high-explosive shells dig are like the craters which stud the sides of an active volcano-showed everywhere in the fields. The cemeteries had been forced to give up their dead, and the bones dug up by the shells flung, as if in derision of all piety, along the surface of the tortured soil. Here a skull showed, there almost a complete skeleton, there again just a fragment of bone.

As for buildings, in some places they hardly existed longer. To instance Nieuport, the most considerable town of the devastated district (not now a port, but deserted, like its greater neighbour, Bruges, by the sea). Nieuport has not suffered as much as Dixmude. It has suffered more than Ramscappelle and about as much as Pervyse. It represents about the average of the destruction of the towns. In Nieuport, with its thousands of houses, not one is altogether undamaged. Quite half are absolutely destroyed. There is no street which has not its heap of ruins. Some streets are nothing but ruins. Of the churches, the chief one, a fine Gothic building almost as large as Westminster Abbey, has some of its outer walls standing. Inside it is a ruin of stones, bricks, glass, slates, human bones, charred wood. The very vaults have been torn open by the German shells, and the relics of the dead thrown up to the sun. One hillock of ruins within the church walls was twenty feet high: one crater of a shell was twelve feet deep. Three other churches have suffered ruin, though not such complete ruin.

Of the Hôtel de Ville a façade survives, but the roof has gone, and one side-wall and all the interior walls have been blown to ruin. The convents, the schools, the other public buildings are more or less destroyed, and the greater majority of the private houses. Sometimes a house took the blow of the shell squarely, and remains now as a heap of bricks and timber cumbering the street. Sometimes it had a glancing blow, and one side only was destroyed. To look at a house of two storeys with its front cut off by a shell and its interior revealed, as it were, in section, brought with it a suggestion of an almost indelicate curiosity.

The continuous bombardment, of course, killed very many of the civilian population who had not fled. There was safety nowhere, neither in cellars nor behind walls, from such intense shell-fire. But I encountered one citizen who had lived with his wife and three children throughout the whole bombardment (it lasted in its full intensity ten days, and on other days the town came under shell-fire). He was standing guard over his ruined house, indignant that to the damage of the shells some addition had been made by the soldiers in occupation, but proud of his feat of endurance and eager to show the photographs of his wife and children.

A brave citizen, certainly, with that stubbornness of courage which you find sometimes in the pronounced "cit" type. He was not robust at all; a prosperous little trader, or a semi-professional man; perhaps a clerk or a photographer. In his own home, before the war, one might picture him as something of a kindly tyrant, worshipped by his wife, often dreaming of great adventures, but conscious that he must be careful against colds in winter. And when the German attack came he was resolute that no savage invader would make him flee from his home. It was his home and there he would stay; and, with supreme confidence in the house-father, wife and children stayed with him during those ten days of destruction and horror, and all escaped death.

A useless feat of courage? No; these things tell for the character of a nation. When that citizen of Nieuport has a group portrait taken of his family in front of his shell-pierced house-as he inevitably will-the picture will be worthy of a place in the gallery of the brave.

The sight of this battlefield was not cheerful, with the question which it conjured up as to whether this was to be the fate of other parts of Belgium in tearing them back from the grip of the Germans.

Nor was it cheerful to think that after all this slaughter there was no very definite result of the battle of the Yser. I noted on November 7th:

"Here, on the Yser, after many days of slaughter and many nights of trench life, we have beaten the German invaders to a standstill. After their efforts to advance had been utterly broken we began on our part an advance, meeting at first with but feeble resistance. But we had not force enough left for the effort to beat down the rallied German defence. Now, the Battle of the Yser, won once, is to be fought all over again. We are back in our old position the Germans back in theirs. Probably, as the war develops, positions such as was the position at the Yser last week will recur frequently. Those who wish to see the war ended quickly will work to secure that they will not develop as this one did, on stalemate lines, but will be preliminaries to decisive victories won by new troops flung in at the proper time. These new troops must come ultimately from the British reservoir, for it is the only one on the western theatre of the war that has not been very heavily drawn upon as yet. The moral to be urged of this past week is that whilst we cannot repair the past we can safeguard the future.

"A new battle on the old battlefield, besides its suggestion of waste of life, will have many circumstances of horror. The area on both sides of the Yser between the sea and Dixmude is already sodden with carnage. Hardly a house, hardly an acre of it but has been ravaged by shell-fire. The slain animals-the oxen of the field and the horses of the army-stay where they have fallen. The whole area almost is water-logged with brackish water, because of the defensive inundations of the Belgians; and in the marshes, in the mud, in the overflowing canals, in the watercourses and trenches are bodies of men and of horses which must be left without burial.

"It is not likely that over this dismal battlefield the Germans will make any progress. But the pity of it is that the same area should be the field of battle again, instead of our troops having the inspiration of pushing on towards Ostend."

The weather, too, in early November, was more severe than I have ever known it in mid-winter in England. The Flanders marshes, frozen iron-hard, swept by a bitter wind from the hated East, recalled the Canadian prairie in December. But the Belgian officers at work in the trenches persisted in taking a patriotic view of the weather. "This will be good," they would say, "for our friends the Russians: and it is better for the English fleet – is it not? – that the weather should be clear rather than foggy."

The hope of an advance on our part in November was baffled by the development of a strong German attack on Ypres. Having failed to break through at Dixmude-Nieuport towards Calais, the Germans now made a desperate effort to find a way by Ypres. That effort was gloriously checked by the British troops. But the story of it does not come within the scope of this book, and was not within the range of my direct observations, though echoes of it reached us in our little Belgian town behind the Yser.

Of life in that town an impression written on November 24th:

"Our little town is at the back of the Belgian Army. It has been bombarded more than once. At one time it was almost abandoned by the civil people, because the Germans were expected to break through. But, all things considered, it enjoys a high measure of comfort compared with other towns within the war area. It has never actually lacked food, never been pillaged, never seen its dead unburied, its streets in flames. Life here is not exactly gay; but it is endurable. It gives matter for reflection that so much of the comforts of civilization can be so easily dispensed with.

"In effect we are back, here, at least two centuries. There are no telegraphs or telephones, except for the use of the army; and that use is confined strictly to military needs. A general's wife, the other day, seeking to know the fate of her husband, not more than fifty miles away, was given no expectation of getting her news within less than a week. The post-office is also suspended. There is no certainty that a letter, even one sent with the sanction of the military authorities, will be despatched.

It may be submitted for approval, endorsed for despatch, stamped, consigned to the military post-office. Afterwards its fate is uncertain. Perhaps it will reach its destination after a week or two; perhaps not.

"No newspaper is published here. Papers from other towns filter in, generally by way of the hospitals. Such things as magazines, reviews, books, are unknown as articles of commerce, but can be got now and again as a matter of favour. There are shops open, however, and the things one can buy and one cannot buy can be set out in curious contrast. Some non-essential things, the *débris* of luxury, can be bought or had for the asking. Some once-essential comforts are lacking. It is easy to buy a stove, impossible to buy coal or wood. Perfumes are in good stock, antiseptics unobtainable. Little articles of feminine adornment abound; but warm underclothing, towels, blankets, may not be had for money. A large stock of tinned peas and tinned asparagus exists; but no jam, cocoa, chocolate, tea, biscuits, tinned fish, tinned meats, nor bacon. Fresh meat, bread, some root vegetables grown locally are still on sale; but butter and cheese are lacking. For a long while there was no tobacco: now the coarse shag issued to the troops is available, but neither cigars, cigarettes, nor English pipe tobacco.'

"One of our stock recreations is to forage for food supplies. Occasionally in some out-of-the-way shop the search of diligence is rewarded by the discovery of something eatable, a tin of preserved fruit, a forgotten remnant of some sweetmeat, a little stock of sugar; or, most precious of all, a bottle of mineral water. (The town water supply is more than suspect, and the lack of pure drinking water is probably the greatest hardship.) There is a resident of the town who is seen sometimes eating an egg.

It gives him almost celebrity. The source of supply is kept as a grand secret. One suspects that he has a private hen somewhere concealed in his room.

"Occasionally from our town someone on official business goes to London, a city where things can be bought (though in a dim light), of which we keep memories. He comes back with strange tales of the perils of the path, the posts which must be passed, with repeated and minute examination of papers, the ordeals of search which must be endured, the passage across the mined Channel, the traverse of Kent by trains whose lights are shrouded.

"The daring voyager comes back, too, with some supplies, if he has a heart of compassion, but never with enough supplies. There are at least thirty people with some claim on his courtesy who expect to find in his pockets boots and shirts and socks, and sweaters and great coats, and sardines and plum puddings, and cigarettes and jam, and biscuits and writing-paper, and envelopes and books, and papers and mineral water and cake. For three days after his return he is made unhappy with reproachful glances. Then it is forgotten that he has been to London.

"There is another city called Paris, separated from us by a hundred posts, demanding papers and pink *laisser-parsers* and blue *laisser-passers,* and photographs and the like. But it is not generally suspected that things can be bought in Paris, though surely some shops survive there. Coming back from Paris-if any one ever does come back-the voyager is not expected to bring supplies. Of the rest of the world we have no actual cognizance. That railways still run, that newspapers are still published, affairs of manufacture and commerce still move elsewhere, we have no certainties; merely suspicions founded on indirect evidence. We have plunged back into the outlook of the seventeenth century; without posts, without newspapers, without any certainty of communication.

"One joy and privilege of the seventeenth century has come back – the social life of the town square. By keeping in touch with the town square one can feel the pulse of the world beating. It is a newspaper and a salon and a popular café, all in one. Soldiers passing to and fro tell by their confidence, as they march towards the enemy, that things are going well; or by their stern, set faces as they go back from the front that things are not so well; gossips go around telling the wonderful stories of the war, always interesting, if rarely true. The officials who know facts and are willing to impart them to discreet ears, pass to and fro. There is even a little pink thread of gossip of a semi-scandalous kind; and apparitions occasionally of dames of fashion. These apparitions are followed sometimes by proclamations or orders of the day unfavourable to such apparitions in the future.*

Frivolity is not encouraged.

"Occasionally our town square is filled with pomp and music when there is a grand review of troops by some European ruler or great general. Once King Albert and General Joffre reviewed a division of troops which had come from far-off Verdun to the Yser.

Again on November 2nd the President of the French Republic visited the Belgian Army in our town, and in his honour a review of some squadrons of Belgian and French cavalry

*On November 16th I learnt that rigorous official action was being taken in regard to various semi-official or private hospital organizations which had sent detachments to the theatre of war. The cold official view was that to some hospital helpers the war was really regarded in the light of an interesting theatrical performance or as a means to obtain furtively facilities, which would not be granted on open application, to see operations. At the time there was a certain amount of reason for the official anger-hospital organizations which could be suspected of having the care of the wounded as a secondary object. There were flitting about the lines numbers of ladies who did a great deal of travelling for a very little nursing. Unconvinced, seemingly, of the grand seriousness of this war, they sought at the front relaxation from the dullness of London, and the fact that in the main their intentions were good and that incidentally they did a certain amount of useful work, did not prevent them from being an embarrassment to the generals in the field.

regiments was held. This interlude in the stern business of war was by chance very happily timed, for it had been arranged for a day on which the fatigue which oppressed the German Army had allowed some respite to our army. Nevertheless, no infantry could be spared from the trenches. The heroic Belgian Army was represented only by a regiment of cavalry. The honour was well merited by them of standing before the President of France to speak for their comrades. These Belgian Lancers did yeoman work at the outset of the war as daring scouts, as intrepid patrols, as dashing pursuers of a beaten enemy. Much of the credit of the fine operations around Tirlemont, after the fall of Liége, and of the attacks which the Belgian Army made from out of Antwerp, belongs to them ; and when occasion called they cheerfully set aside their horses and put in a critical week in the trenches, acting as infantry.

"The sky smiled on the ceremony. The day was of pearl with a hint of rose and of gold. The most typical towns of Flanders-Bruges, Ghent, Alost, Termonde (alas! now no more!), seem to have been designed by their architects in the Middle Ages for the setting of that atmosphere of pearl touched with rose. The square this morning was a gem of elegant, of pensive beauty. As it began to be lined with the cavalry and a thin fringe of townspeople (a great part of the population fled during a bombardment the previous day), the national music of Flanders resounding from the steeples of the churches made the air vibrant with joy; and the savage battles, the blood-soaked trenches, were almost forgotten for an hour in giving welcome to the Ruler of a friendly nation, which in the harsh struggle of 1870 refused to seek safety by treachery to Belgium, which now in 1914 was striving with all its manhood to atone the wrongs done to Belgium because she in her turn was faithful to her word.

"But the war could not be quite forgotten. As the town square awaited its guest, a rude reminder came. A Taube, eluding our air scouts and soaring over the town at a great height, dropped a bomb. It missed the square, and spent its murderous rage harmlessly on a building near the railway station.

Not a soldier in the ranks flinched. The parade calmly waited. A fine mettle of courage it proved to stand thus in a town which yesterday was systematically shelled. It recalled the heroes of the *Birkenhead*; but one could not help thinking that the peril to the brave troops was too great a price to pay for a courtesy.

"At nine a regiment of French cavalry took their position in the square with a flourish of trumpets, and the assemblage of troops was complete. The premature and vain malice of the Germans had awakened to the strictest vigilance our air scouts. With the joyous music from the steeples and from the bands came constantly the hum of their wings as they patrolled around and around the circle of the square, like eagles on guard. A spectacle of a lifetime this square now: framed around with gallant troops; its seventeenth century towers, crowned with tiny minarets in the shape of candle-flames, showing like nacre in the gentle October sun; triumphant, crashing music of bells and trumpets giving defiance to the enemy: and overhead the soaring guardians in the sky.

"A review of soldiers who have not been in action, who are really but postulants in the order of chivalry, will never again have any savour, no matter what their number, their bearing, their equipment, after seeing on parade warriors fresh from the field of battle, with the pride of their struggles shining from their eyes and their resolution for the future showing on their brows.

"Enter the President of France in civilian dress, the King of Belgium in the undress uniform of general. To the music of the 'Marseillaise'-beneath every note as a motif was the hum of the aeroplanes saying 'security'-they drove around the square, inspecting the troops. At ten the troops left the square, and no incident of slaughter had marked the challenge which they had given to German malice. Fortunate conclusion to a morning of lofty courage and chivalrous courtesy! It came with something of reassurance and hope, as suggesting the dawn of the day of victory for the cause of civilization. All the malice of the German invader had failed to disturb this parade of the Allies in the very teeth of the batteries which were shelling the town the previous day.

"Of course in our town there are anxieties, dangers, doubts. Never a day, rarely an hour, without its funeral of some brave soul. Sometimes there comes the fear that the term has not yet been set to the invader's march, and that fresh sacrifices have yet to be made. Withal, life here is not unhappy. We have at least three fine buildings to look upon. The simple necessities of life are provided, and one learns what can be done without."

Still it was not a position of undisturbed security at ———. Sometimes we heard of a new German effort contemplated on the Yser. For example, on November 9th this document fell into our hands:

Report of the Commandant of the 38th Brigade, Landw., to the Division of Marine at Bruges:

Following the verbal order concerning an attack projected against Nieuport I report to you as follows:

Nieuport is an old fortress with a fosse filled with water. Coming from the direction of the east one can get in by a passage crossing three swingbridges. The big canals in front of the town are serious obstacles. Over them there are no bridges. Access to the fortress can only be had by roads commanded by the enemy's fire and crossing heavily-inundated areas.

The fortress would appear to have for its garrison a division of infantry, with heavy artillery, field artillery, and Maxims. Besides these guns there is in a position covered by the canal leading to the sea a heavy battery and a field battery.

To the south of the town a trench for infantry, strongly held, stretches almost to the fortress. To the south-east of this locality there is a heavy battery and a battery of automobile traction.

The heavy guns of the English fleet have a range almost up to the town and can enfilade the territory on the line of advance in a most efficacious way.

In view of all this I consider that the attack of the fortress from the east is not possible with any chance of success unless the artillery of the defence is completely reduced to silence, the fire of the English fleet also silenced, and the infantry making the attack is greatly superior in numbers.

To obtain artillery superiority the assailants can dispose only of two guns of fifteen centimetres to the south-west of Westende, and two field batteries.

There can be no question of sending sappers in advance to destroy the gates of the fortress and to destroy the obstacles if the troops of the 4th Division of Ersatz (two battalions and two batteries of field artillery) rejoin their unit today.

Therefore I think that an attack on Nieuport with the troops placed at my disposition (33th Brigade Landw., detachment von Bernuth-two battalions of which are at Leffinghe-and one detachment from the Ostend garrison) ought to be considered impossible at the moment.

Reconnaissance patrols sent towards the fortress have been always repulsed by the violent fire of the defence. They will be nevertheless continued.

(Signed) VON KOTZE.

But on the whole it was clear that the German was sick of the Yser. As the days shortened towards December it appeared that he was sick, too, of Ypres. The thin khaki line had held as it held in the red-coated days. The Germans, unable to capture Ypres, were content to destroy its lovely buildings by a long-range bombardment. This began on November 2nd, and has continued with intermissions since. Hardly anything of historic Ypres survives.

Before November had closed it was possible to record:

"There is no longer any reason to doubt that the German movement on their right wing is failing. What has been happening ever since the fall of Antwerp and the sudden German rush down Belgium as far as a line Nieuport-Lichtervelde-Roulers-Menin-Lille, is that the German General Staff has been aiming to take possession of the coast district of Belgium and Northern France, so as to bring their line down to Boulogne-Lille. To fulfil this aim they have been willing to take any route. To pierce through the defence of the Allies at Nieuport and Furnes would have been more valuable, perhaps, than by Ypres – Wormhoudt. But either road, once opened, would have led to complete success. If Dunkirk had been occupied by a strong German force any of the Allied forces left at Nieuport-Furnes would have been isolated, to be destroyed at leisure.

"Thus, almost every point of the line stretching from Nieuport through Ypres to Armentieres was tried in the effort to break through. It can be said with confidence that every effort has failed.

"Reviewing the operations as a whole, they bear a curious resemblance in one particular to the first week of the campaign. Again the German Army has suffered a severe check because it treated – as it did at Liége-the Belgian Army as a negligible factor. Now, as around Liége, the Belgians, by sticking to their ground against odds, have saved valuable days, and this time they have enabled enough forces to be brought up to turn the tide of invasion back. In their first plan the Germans devoted only a poor ten thousand troops to the task of turning towards the coast from Ghent to chase the Belgian Army into the sea. The bulk of the force from Antwerp went down south towards Ypres. But the German coast force found that the Belgian Army, as soon as overwhelming pressure was removed, could turn.

The Belgians first checked, then beat back the Germans past Ostend. At once the German plan was modified, and a force reaching at one stage, it is said, to one hundred and fifty thousand, was collected to march down the coast to Calais, sweeping aside the Belgian Army and then getting ready to swing around and face any movement of the Allies from the east. Probably in the early stages of the Battle of the Yser the German force was quite sixty thousand at that point. Afterwards it was greater.

"On October 18th, the Belgian Army, by its leaders, was urged to hold the position of the Yser until the 20th, when sufficient aid would come to enable the men to have a rest. This appeal came to an army which had done more than two months' retreat-fighting, and which was supposed (by other than German critics) to be only capable of going into winter quarters at once for reorganization for the spring. But the men to whom it was made held on not only until the 20th, but until many days after, and on the 1st of November were equal to the task of turning the Germans back with a bayonet charge. Truly the Germans miscalculated seriously! Of course, the Belgian Army was not left without aid all that time. The British naval aid was the most prompt, and it helped to shatter the enemy's artillery superiority. French aid was rushed forward as speedily as possible, and in the later stages of the combat of the Yser it was a genuinely international rampart which stood in the way of the German invader. But the chief credit must go to the Belgian Army."

"Forgetting the Belgians" has been a great fault of the Germans in this war. I hope it will not be a fault of Europe in making the peace.

THE END

APPENDIX:

THE POSITION OF THE WAR CORRESPONDENT

FROM August 5th to November 25th I was able to follow the fortunes of the Belgian Army, and to reconcile myself to postponing gratification of the natural wish, when one's own country is at war, to take part in, rather than to describe, the fighting, with the thought that since a campaign must have its current record I was doing a useful work. At some times – such as the occasion of the Zeppelin attack on Antwerp – I felt fairly confident on that point. But work as war correspondent became more and more difficult and unpleasant as the campaign proceeded. Both the British and French authorities treated the war correspondent as something nearly equivalent to a spy.

The existing regulations of the British Army in the field provide that war correspondents attached to the force must wear green armlets and must not employ captive balloons. By the side of this heartless prohibition of captive balloons-what war correspondent would dream of going towards the front without his captive balloon? – it is a comparatively minor matter that the war correspondent is absolutely prohibited from approaching the British lines at all, the penalty being expulsion from the country to England under military detention.

This regulation about captive balloons suggests that the British War Office intends one day to relax its present stern prohibition and allow accredited correspondents to accompany the Army in the field. But the position as it is at present seems not likely to be changed for a little while and may be discussed as if it were stable.

Taking the various countries at war *seriatim,* Germany has no independent war correspondents at the front; some Dutch and American journalists and photographers are tolerated, but not allowed, evidently, to see operations. Russia seems to have adopted the policy of "feeding" correspondents with plenty of matter from the front; but no correspondent is actually seeing operations, so far as one can judge, or allowed any opportunity to check what he is told. Austria follows the same policy as Germany. France forbids journalists to enter her lines, but lately has been conducting tours of journalists over old battlefields. Great Britain follows the French policy. Belgium has been kinder to the journalists than any of the belligerents, and has tolerated, indeed encouraged, friendly journalists in the lines.

That is the position summarized. But in practical working the prohibition of correspondents by Great Britain has not proved rigid. A cloud of British correspondents have followed the British and French armies at a distance, taking opportunities to slip in near the lines and to the lines, and collect "stories." When discovered they have been expelled. But with reasonable luck discovery was not very likely.

This method of journalism, with its atmosphere of masquerade and furtiveness, cannot be held to be dignified. It is unworthy of the old high tradition of the British press and must be disquieting, if not actually disgusting, to journals and journalists asked to take part in it. But in a measure it has been forced on the newspapers. The ultimate responsibility for it rests with the authority which makes a rule and then keeps it so ineffectively that it can be ignored at the sacrifice of some scrupulousness. If the British authority honestly believes that it is advisable that no news of the operations of the British Army, no description of its work, except such as is supplied officially, should be published, there is a simple way of effecting that end : prohibit the publication of all "stories" from the British and French lines. Then to elude the vigilance of authority would be useless, for no benefit would be gained.

But that is not done; and the fact that it is not done suggests that there is a doubt as to whether the official attitude about war correspondents is quite wise. Of course, if the safety of the nation demanded the suppression of all news of the war except such as the official bulletin chose to tell there would be no wisdom in trying to argue the point. The liberty of the Press is a great thing: the safety of the Empire is a greater. But I claim that no harm need come and much good should come from a wisely-regulated, independent press service at the front. The best of official *communiqués*, the most eloquent of official accounts, cannot serve the same purpose as independent accounts.

Even if my claim is not allowed, no one, surely, will refuse to agree that the present policy is bad, of making a Draconic law and then encouraging its evasion. It recalls the Spartans being encouraged to steal though punished when discovered stealing. So long as the sin of being found out is avoided, the newspaper correspondent who has got near to the lines can nearly always reap the reward for his paper of a "story" which has at least some atmosphere of truth, however absurdly exaggerated it may be, and is therefore superior in value to the story written frontiers away on the basis of a feather moulted from the wing of Rumour.

It would seem, however, that British authority may one day admit that the total suppression of the Liberty of the Press as regards the war operations is not wise. If authority feels that some independent description and comment is advisable (there have been many incidents of the war suggesting that it is advisable), here is a suggestion for a limited authorization to war correspondents under regulations safeguarding against abuse:

1. Only such correspondents to be authorized as are citizens of Great Britain or of nations allied to Great Britain acting solely for journals published within the territories of the Allies.

2. Good personal character of the correspondent and good character of his newspaper to be conditions of authorization as correspondent.

3. Before being authorized every correspondent to submit to an examination and to prove that he has an elementary knowledge of military conditions and military law, and good discretion.

4. Every accredited correspondent then to be granted temporary rank as sub-lieutenant during his attachment to the army, thus bringing him under military law and facilitating punishment of any indiscretion, misbehaviour, or treason.

5. As additional precautions a vigilant and instructed censorship at the front and at the home base.

With these restrictions it would be impossible for any grave abuses to occur. The men at the front would be men of character and discretion. They would be under military law and under careful censorship. Normally they would be able to send to their newspapers accounts which would not be dangerous to the public good, but which would foster patriotic enthusiasm and would help to a real knowledge of the war. Under abnormal conditions they would be watch-dogs for the public against abuses. A war correspondent of this type would have no temptation to attempt any factitious criticisms. But he would be some check on any development at the front of sloth, or any grave neglect by the Home authority of the soldiers' interest. One does not want to see a war conducted as if it were a General Election amid a fierce cross-fire of criticism; but there can be imagined circumstances when independent knowledge of what is going on should be available to the public.

So far as my personal experience is affected I did not join in any furtive news-snatching expeditions, but tried (with the warm support of my Belgian friends) to be a "regular" war correspondent. The attempt broke down when the Belgian operations came within the sphere of British authority. The event showed that the British Government at the moment was unalterably hostile not only to possible abuses by war correspondents but to any independent despatches. This is the record, in brief, of my experience.

At the outbreak of the war I was asked by the Morning Post to follow the fortunes of the Belgian Army in the field; travelled to Brussels, and after an interval of some days (which I judged necessary to arrive at an understanding of the real position, much confused by sensational reports) began work.

Subsequent strict reticence about matters which would give the enemy knowledge of our *terrain* in Belgium and hints of our defensive dispositions was (I believe) acknowledged by the British Censor.

The Belgian authorities made no objection at all to the issue of a *laisser-passer* giving full rights of movement. Belgian officers in the field were more than courteous. As soon as it was understood that I had had some little military experience I was allowed to go everywhere and was able to observe all operations and communicate something about German tactics and strategy. All despatches were submitted to the Belgian censorship. There were numberless ways of evading that censorship with despatches; but I never tried any. I took the view that a war correspondent had a duty to the army to which he was attached as well as to his paper.

Just before the fall of Brussels I learned (from a French journalist) that "the British Government had issued orders for the expulsion of all war correspondents." He was very bitter about this interference on the part of the British Government with French journalists. Doubting the correctness of his impression, I called at the British Ministry. An official there courteously communicated to me the exact position. The British Government had intimated to the Belgian Government its desire that war correspondents should not be allowed with the Belgian Army, but had given no orders.

Seeking to know the Belgian attitude, I was informed at the Ministry for War by a responsible official that the Belgian Government had no wish to expel friendly journalists. He was good enough to add that in my case they would be very sorry that I should go, saying something complimentary regarding my despatches.

Under these circumstances I decided to stay with the Belgian Army, awaiting instructions from my Editor.

Brussels was occupied by the Germans shortly after. I escaped out of the city on the arrival of the Germans on a bicycle, crossing the frontier into Holland. At the earliest opportunity I rejoined the Belgian Army Headquarters at Antwerp. In Holland it was reported most explicitly that Antwerp was then besieged and starving. Arriving at Antwerp-for some time I was the only British correspondent there-I was able to report on the falsity of these accounts and to communicate matter which was held to be very useful as to the true position of the Belgian Army and the attitude of Holland *vis-à-vis* Belgium.

In Antwerp I had a warm greeting from the Belgian État-Major. Submitting, of course, all despatches to censorship, I was favoured with great telegraphic facilities. At the time of the first Zeppelin attack on the city I was (I understand) the only British correspondent in the city. Some messages were sent by my means to American journals of influence from a United States citizen in Antwerp, which had the effect of arousing United States public opinion on the subject of the Zeppelin atrocities. I mention the fact as one of many incidents when an independent war correspondent was useful to the army to which he was attached.

Antwerp being a fortress, every stranger was required to have a "permission to stay" (over and above the *laisser-passer* I already had). To get this permission it was necessary to have a formal certificate from the British Minister that I was a "reputable person." This certificate was refused to me on instructions from the British Government. I was thus put in the position of being a "disreputable person" who should be expelled. I intimated to the Belgian authorities, repeatedly in conversation and twice in writing, that I was prepared to leave at any moment on their request. The request never came. Their wish that I should stay was repeatedly expressed. An official intimation of the high view taken as to the usefulness of my despatches confirmed my Editor in the decision that I should stay.

As a "disreputable person" refused a certificate by my Government I stayed in Antwerp, allowed by the Belgian authorities full access everywhere, constantly with the fighting troops, getting independent testimony of German misdeeds and some further knowledge of German tactics. On one occasion, in spite of my "disreputable" position, I was appealed to by a British Government Department for further information about events at Aerschot.

I stayed at Antwerp until the end of the bombardment; then escaped to Flushing by the river as the Germans entered the city. From Flushing I went to London; thence to Calais, and thence to the new headquarters of the Belgian Army. At once I reported to the Belgian État-Major, and by favour of an officer was able to get quarters in an hotel reserved to the Quartier General.

Very strict new regulations had been made. Civilians were not allowed to travel in motor-cars or on bicycles. After a week the concession was made to me that my *laisser-passer* was endorsed to allow me to ride a bicycle. There was no regular censorship, but the Intelligence Officer of the Belgian Quartier General said he would be content if I submitted my despatches to the British

Mission attached to the Quartier General. This I did at first, and my despatches were endorsed and forwarded in the Quartier General mail-bag. Afterwards, to avoid the difficulty that matter passed at —————— would not be passed in London, my despatches were submitted to London censorship only. But I was always more than willing to submit them at —————— too. Belgian officers made no secret of their satisfaction that I was there. Through an accident on November 3rd my position as correspondent came directly under the notice of the British authority in the field. It is not allowed to me to be explicit on this point; but after full inquiry it was decided that, as I had been regularly with the Belgian Army and under no suspicion at any time of any irregularities, I should be allowed to stay at the Belgian Headquarters.

But on November 23rd I was asked to call on the Belgian Provost-Marshal, and was informed "with extreme regret" that I must leave. (The one other correspondent who was openly in —————— received the same intimation. Several other correspondents who were furtively in the town or its vicinity were not affected.) Asking why, I was told that it was the order of the British Government, communicated through the British Mission. I was told emphatically that the Belgian authorities did not wish it. I appealed to the head of the British Mission, insisting that this was going behind the wishes of the Belgian authorities and behind a recent decision of the highest British authority in the field. He agreed to refer the matter to the Adjutant-General. The next day I received a verbal message that the decision was unchanged.

The position thus was that the British Government, without being able to allege the slightest irregularity on my part, forced the Belgian authority to take an action which it regretted and which it regarded as not consistent with its best interests. The position of the Belgian Government was, of course, just then, not one which allowed it to be stiff against the orders of a powerful friend; and I could see no use in adding to its troubles by appealing to it. Besides I was personally glad to be relieved of newspaper duty so as to volunteer for active service. But the British Government attitude should be made clear, that not only does it refuse to allow correspondents with its army, but it forced the Belgian Government to send away a correspondent without alleging misconduct, folly, or indiscretion.

It is an attitude which is not easy to understand and which will make the task of the future historian of the war a very difficult one. Tacit encouragement is given to the ornate: (but fictional) "stories" written from towns remote from the front: the most complete veto possible is put on careful and discreet observation.

I dare to hope that this book, a record of my experiences with the Belgian Army, will not provide another argument against the war correspondent.

THE AUTHOR.